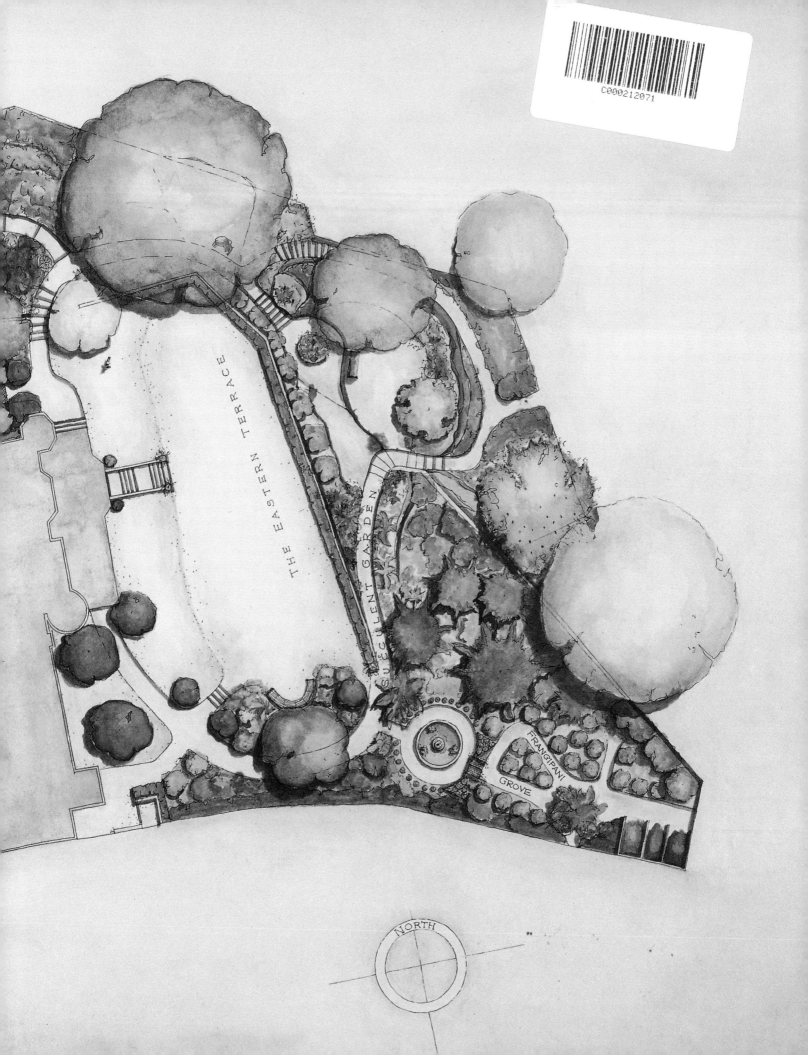

THE EASTERN TERRACE

SUCCULENT GARDEN

FRANGIPANI GROVE

NORTH

Leo Schofield

Brook House
2002.

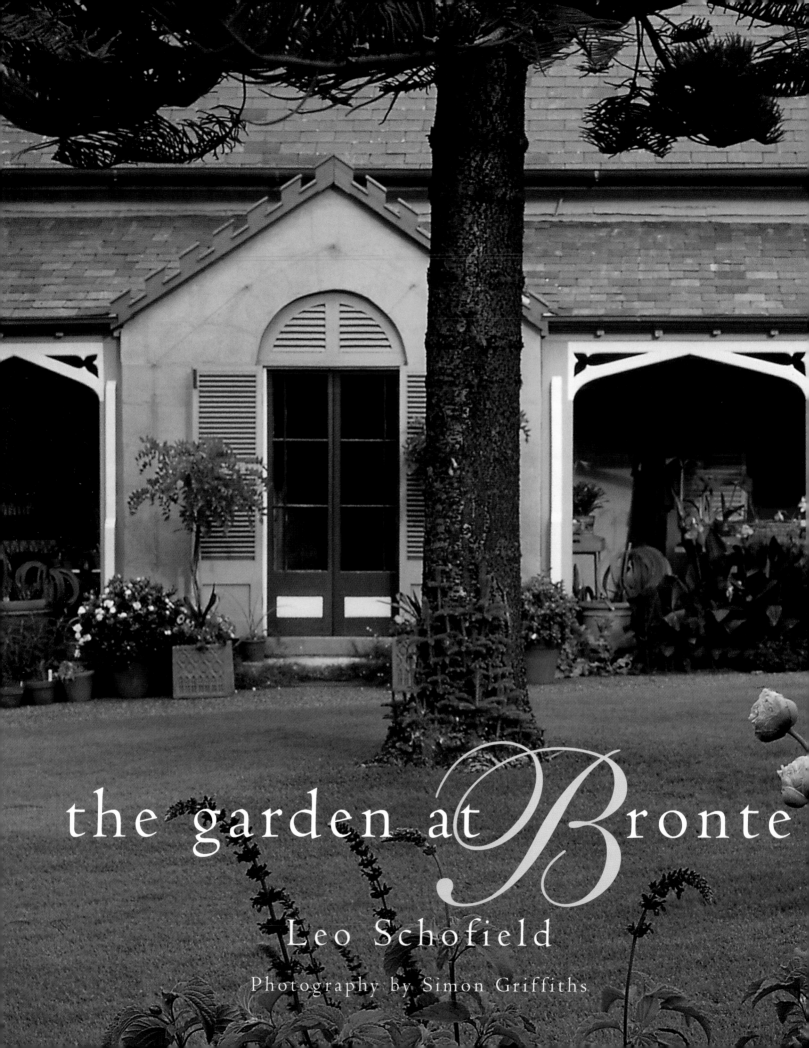

the garden at Bronte

Leo Schofield

Photography by Simon Griffiths

VIKING

Since February 1995 a number of gardeners
have worked at Bronte House. Brendan Lewis
was the first and stayed for five years. The
current health of the garden is due in large
measure to his efforts. His successor, Myles
Baldwin, has brought to it a rare combination
of horticultural awareness, design sensitivity
and daring. Steve Putnam worked for the
previous lessees and continues to be involved
from time to time. To all three this book is
gratefully dedicated.

Endpapers Watercolour plan of the garden at Bronte House by Alexandra Shepherd.

Extract from the *Australian Town and Country Journal* circa 1860, *page 22*,
held in the State Reference Library, State Library of New South Wales.

Watercolours by Georgiana Lowe circa 1845, *pages 25, 29 (top left), 30 and 32*,
reproduced by permission the Library Council of New South Wales.

Excerpts from the letters of Georgiana Lowe circa 1845, *pages 26, 31, 32 and 33*,
held in the Mitchell Library, State Library of New South Wales.

Sketch *page 33* reproduced by permission the Dixson Galleries, State Library
of New South Wales.

Photographs *page 114 and 164* courtesy Lorrie Graham.

Photographs *page 157 and 158 (bottom)* courtesy Brent Wilson.

Viking

Published by the Penguin Group
Penguin Books Australia Ltd
250 Camberwell Road, Camberwell, Victoria 3124, Australia
Penguin Books Ltd
80 Strand, London WC2R 0RL, England
Penguin Putnam Inc.
375 Hudson Street, New York, New York 10014, USA
Penguin Books, a division of Pearson Canada
10 Alcorn Avenue, Toronto, Ontario, Canada M4V 3B2
Penguin Books (NZ) Ltd
Cnr Rosedale and Airborne Roads, Albany, Auckland, New Zealand
Penguin Books (South Africa) (Pty) Ltd
24 Sturdee Avenue, Rosebank, Johannesburg 2196, South Africa
Penguin Books India (P) Ltd
11, Community Centre, Panchsheel Park, New Delhi 110 017, India

First published by Penguin Books Australia 2002

10 9 8 7 6 5 4 3 2 1

Cover and text designed by Nikki Townsend, Penguin Design Studio
Digital enhancement of cover images by Splitting Image
Typeset in 11pt Berkeley by Nikki Townsend, Penguin Design Studio,
and Post Pre-press Group, Brisbane, Queensland
Printed and bound in Singapore by Imago Productions

National Library of Australia
Cataloguing-in-Publication data:

Schofield, Leo George 1935– .
   The garden at Bronte.

   ISBN 0 670 87866 9.

   1. Historic gardens – New South Wales – Sydney.
   2. Landscape gardening – New South Wales – Sydney.
   3. Gardens – New South Wales – Sydney.
   I. Griffiths, Simon, 1966– .
   II. Title.

712.6099441

www.penguin.com.au

contents

introduction

This is the chronicle of a work in progress, the eight-year rehabilitation of a garden. But because the garden and the house it surrounds are inextricably linked, it is also necessary to include something of the history of the latter.

So, gentle reader, if you are not interested in who lived here first, how they came to choose this spot above others, the ups and downs of the place, the various attempts at subdivision and the miracle of its survival, you may wish to fast-forward to the chapters that deal with practical matters such as digging and planting, trial and error, triumphs and failures, propagation, seed-gathering, cutting-taking, pruning, shaping, clipping, raking, weeding, path-making, hedging, potting, composting and the other tasks that make the difference between an area of token green and an attractive garden.

This has been not so much a project as a mission. In assorted newspaper columns and articles over the past three decades, I've berated public authorities for their lack of interest in the cultivated landscape. If a space outside a suburban house in Sydney is well kept, you can be certain that the local authority has had no hand in it. The homeowner will have mown the verge and maintained trees initially planted by councils and then abandoned. We are not a nation of gardeners. Gardening is hard work and is mostly carried out in leisure time, and in Australia there are other more seductive calls on our leisure time – the beach, footy, television, parties. Most people are interested in gardens, but as *voyeurs*, not active participants in the process of enhancing their personal spaces. They take pleasure in admiring the handiwork of others but feel no urge to go forth and do likewise. Admiring other people's gardens is one thing; making one yourself is another, and I have long wanted to make a singular garden. My early efforts were mere dry runs for this one.

At one stage in my life I dreamed of a romantic old house in Tasmania. At other times I have ached for a house by the sea in, say, Far North Queensland. But, being an urban animal, I have also felt the need of the attractions and stimulation of a metropolis. At Bronte House I have it all: a house of the kind one might easily find in Tasmania, overlooking the ocean and within a whistle of central Sydney. But most importantly, it has a significant garden. Thus have all my ambitions been simultaneously achieved.

There are times here when it is so quiet and still that one could conceivably be in the bush or in distant Tassie. And on warm evenings, when the scents from the garden invade the house and envelop it, along with its inhabitants and guests, it is not hard to imagine oneself in the tropics. For the time being, for the extent of my lease, I live in the best of all possible worlds.

I am a committed garden visitor and have seen many marvels, from the Villa Gamberaia overlooking Florence, to Villandry in France and Hidcote in England, but the most exciting garden I have ever visited – and I have done so on numerous occasions – is the so-called Center Garden at the new Getty Center in Los Angeles. This was designed not by your conventional landscape architect but by an artist, a Southern Californian abstract expressionist painter called Robert Irwin. Of his work he wrote: 'If you are going to experience a garden in all of its qualities, you have to keep coming back. A garden is a commitment.'

For the past eight years the garden at Bronte has been my commitment. Wholeheartedly.

Leo Schofield
Bronte, November 2002

'a little estate by the sea'

This garden! Few visitors are impervious to its charms. It is not big, nor is it grand and formal, and its plan is somewhat haphazard. Only a single hectare of the original seventeen remains and many of its once distinctive features have vanished. Nonetheless it is seductive, irresistible. It billows towards you, comes at you with a rush as if to welcome you into its cool, green embrace.

first sight

In 1845, when the house was built and the garden begun, visitors approaching on horseback or in carriages travelled gingerly downhill in a gentle series of zigs and zags along a road cut from virgin bush. At that time of sparse population, many houses could be seen from a distance and approached in leisurely fashion, coming into sharper focus the closer one came. Not this one. Both house and garden were invisible from the road, masked by trees along the drive. However, there was a particular point, a sharp turn in the road, at which both hove suddenly and dramatically into view. So it is today.

Then, one would have turned off the dirt road to confront a neat, wide drive bordering a large roundel of clipped lawn with a Norfolk Island pine planted authoritatively at its heart and, just behind, a long, low, single-storey house of quirky, picturesque design with the blue ocean beyond. Today the theatre of arrival is much the same. One turns a corner and spots the house, although it is now fenced as it never was originally. Instead of sweeping into the circular drive, one now parks and enters through a small gate on the northern side to confront the same house and lawn and tree and that surprising and delightful onward rush of plants.

Most gardens are reticent, slow to reveal their charms immediately. Not this one. A crammed panorama of house and lawn and trees and borders is instantly visible.

PAGES 4–5: The Eastern Terrace (see page 116).

PAGE 6: A modern-day view along The Lovers' Walk, to the north of the house.

PAGE 7: The western façade.

ABOVE: Males of the Holdsworth family, early owners of Bronte House, in a variety of headgear, including top hat, cabbage-tree hats and smoking caps, assembled on the circular lawn at Bronte House, circa 1865. The youngest Holdsworth is showing off his Shetland pony. His nurse waits on the porch.

ABOVE TOP: The western façade of the house as it appears today.

ABOVE BOTTOM: A collection of Grand Tour bronze busts in the dining room. The Grand Tour of Italy was an essential part of an eighteenth-century aristocrat's education. Often they returned with superb collections of antique marbles and ideas for magnificent neo-classical palaces.

The eye darts from one form to another in the beds around the carriageway. Gaps in the circle invite the visitor to plunge further into the garden's secret extremities, to descend paths and stone steps to explore its nether areas, to pass under wire arches to steeply contoured spaces and shady walks so far below that only the chimneys of the house can be glimpsed as one meanders along them. In this swirling landscape of circles and spires and pyramids and convoluted pathways and the flourish of flowers, only the house, a horizontal slab of ochre-washed sandstone, is steady.

Long before I took possession of this house it took possession of my imagination. I saw it first over half a century ago, from a toast-rack tram en route to Bronte Beach for a day of sun and surf. The tram ran along Oxford Street to Taylor Square and Bondi Junction, turned into Bronte Road, travelled through Charing Cross to Albion Street, then into Macpherson Street, and through a cutting in the rock cliffs to the wooden Federation tram shed at the lovely little beach below. The tram tracks couldn't follow Bronte Road, which must be one of the most confusing in Sydney, abruptly veering left, then right, then left, then right again, engineered in the early nineteenth century to facilitate the steep descent by horse-drawn vehicle from level ground to the sea.

After our swim we decided to walk uphill along the lower part of Bronte Road to Charing Cross to catch the tram back to Central Station and, while doing so, I caught my first glimpse of the house I now live in. I remember thinking how romantic its

turrets looked, how curious its form. It must, at that time, have been occupied by the Red Cross, for immediately after the war that organisation had been granted a lease on part of the property and used it as offices.

During the subsequent fifty-something years, I passed it again many, many times, always admiring it, always wondering what lay beyond its fence, within its thick sandstone walls. I can't say that I ever thought of living there – that urge was to come later, and again I remember precisely the moment.

In 1981 Waverley Municipal Council, the owners of the property since 1948, advertised for a tenant. Having commissioned well-known heritage architect Clive Lucas to carry out basic maintenance, Council shied away from further major expenditure and invited tenders from anyone interested in leasing the house and investing in its repair and ongoing maintenance in exchange for a twenty-five-year lease at a peppercorn rental. This arrangement was optimistically viewed as a way to preserve an historic building and garden without hurling vast amounts of ratepayer funds into the bottomless pit of restoration, and the lease, which the National Trust had a hand in drawing up, was to serve as a prototype for similar arrangements for historic properties throughout New South Wales. Soon afterwards, I learned that someone I knew had secured the lease and for the first time I saw the house and garden from the other side of the fence.

ABOVE TOP: The new garage was built in 1982 to a design by Clive Lucas. It stands beside the entry to the drive on the western side.

ABOVE BOTTOM: The formal entrance to the house. At other times a door further along to the right is used. There is a suggestion that during the time Robert and Georgiana Lowe occupied the house (1845–50) this was an open loggia.

the garden at Bronte

the weasel

I first met the mysterious Christopher Selmes in Sydney in the early 1970s and later came to know him a little better in London, where he lived in high style in a splendid house overlooking the Thames in Chelsea. Something of a shady character, he needed, for various reasons, to be out of England most of the year, and the further away the better. Obsessed with food and wine, he had discovered Berowra Waters Inn, possibly the finest restaurant this country has ever seen, and the existence in the Antipodes of such an establishment and Sydney's summer climate were sufficiently potent reasons for him to contemplate an annual sojourn here. At first he stayed in hotels, then he rented a grand house at Palm Beach, but as the notion of recurrent summers in Australia took hold, he began casting about for a permanent bolthole. He found it at Bronte. In 1982 he was

RIGHT: This charming informal photograph shows members of the Ebsworth family assembling for a family wedding party on the front verandah of Bronte House. A lady adjusts a flower in the buttonhole of a gentleman, possibly the groom. Ladies in wasp-waisted gowns with leg o'mutton sleeves wait expectantly on the verandah, while young girls, like prize hens in startlingly white starched cotton and lace, race about and older ladies, widows in black with brollies to match, take up positions on rattan chairs. The fashions suggest a date of about 1895.

declared the successful tenderer for a twenty-five-year lease on the property.

One of the conditions of the lease was that Selmes should spend $200 000 on repairs. He certainly had the wherewithal to do so. The adopted son of a Kent tax collector, he had left school at sixteen to become a stockbroker. By twenty-four he had his own business and a year later he was a millionaire, considered one of the keenest financial brains in London.

But by the time he turned twenty-nine, Selmes was in disgrace. A string of feature stories and editorials in the British press chronicling the collapse of the companies with which he was associated made his ongoing residence there uncomfortable. At the time he signed the twenty-five-year lease on Bronte House, he and his affairs had been under investigation by the UK Department of Trade for four years. When the Department's report was officially issued, Selmes, dubbed 'The Weasel' by the British satirical magazine *Private Eye*, was castigated for dishonesty and misconduct but, like so many swindlers before and after him, he escaped a prison sentence. Just.

The Department of Trade report, released in 1979, ran to 372 pages and was a catalogue of irregular business practices, including bribing people with lavish gifts of Rolls Royces, Cartier watches and Steinway pianos. Some £16 million was involved, secured by a Henry Moore sculpture, shares valued at £16 000 and a promissory note 'binding in honour only' for £116 000.

But all this happened in distant Britain, far from Waverley Council, whose officers knew nothing of Selmes's background. He was declared to be the perfect tenant and signed the lease on the property.

The conditions were not onerous. In addition to the initial expenditure on the building, he was to pay one dollar a year rental, furnish and maintain the property and open it to the public six times a year. In the original lease, Selmes specified the dates of the open days. All were to be held in autumn and winter, when he was elsewhere.

In January 1983 he moved in, but before he did so he invited me over to see his renovations. It was then that I was smitten with a serious case of house envy. Seeing Bronte House from the outside is one thing, but to enter is another.

To architectural purists it's something of a mongrel building. When the drive to Bronte House became a through road in the 1882 subdivision, and one of the four picturesque pepper-pot turrets at each corner was knocked down, an ugly and entirely inappropriate two-storeyed façade to the street was constructed. If one wanted classic architecture, perfection of proportion, elegance, one would look elsewhere, but there is no house I know of in Sydney with the special qualities of this one.

To walk through the entrance of the house was to experience something marvellous and special, for the place had changed little in 150 years. One still entered through two narrow doors into the compressed space of the tiny vestibule with barely

OPPOSITE: Four views of the principal rooms of Bronte House, circa 1895.

TOP LEFT: A view of the dining room that must also have served as a library.

TOP RIGHT: The drawing room, complete with mantelpiece in Belgian slate, family photographs and turn-of-the-century bric-à-brac. The music Canterbury in the corner may have been used for magazines as there is no evidence of a piano.

BOTTOM LEFT: Plush Parian and paisley in the dining room. The white marble fireplace survives with its original grate; whereas the grate in the black chimneypiece in the adjoining drawing room (top right) has been removed by a previous tenant and replaced with a Jetmaster.

BOTTOM RIGHT: The bay window of the dining room with a fitted bench and cushions. That this was a favourite place to loll and read is evidenced by the Holland blinds to exclude harsh sun.

enough room for two people to stand in at any one time. Then one stepped into the east-facing dining room, big and shady, with the marble fireplace and shuttered bay window overlooking the garden. Through another door and an equally beautiful, high-ceilinged drawing room, one was drawn irresistibly by the dazzle of light towards the vast bay window comprising five doors, each with twenty-five small panes and glazing bars terminating in saucy pointed Gothic arches, with a further five similarly small ten-paned windows above, hinged to admit sea breezes. These 175 panes of glistening glass set in a fine web of joinery make one of the loveliest features of the house to this day and lead out onto a wide verandah with commanding views of the Pacific.

Each time I make this modest progress I am still captivated, as is every visitor. There is an element of surprise about the passage, each step providing interest and beguilement. And the garden beyond offers further surprises. Indeed, this house is a place of surprises, of compression and expansion, of vasty rooms and tiny ones, of high ceilings and low, of broad gardens and small, hidden ones. At every turn, there is something to see and admire. And yet it is not awesome. Despite its grandiose name, this house is not grand. It is a simple Regency-style marine villa, a perfect little cottage by the sea, but one with a magic garden that contributes mightily to its appeal.

Today, most of the great colonial houses of Sydney, with the exception perhaps of Carrara, later renamed Strickland House, have been shorn of their curtilages and sit marooned like Georgian whales in a sea of Federation, Art Deco, neo-Tuscan and post-modern minnows, but Bronte House still has a hectare of garden around it. Better still, it is adjacent to a public park to the east, so the feeling of an estate, the sense of peace and privacy, still lingers.

To the east one can see nothing but trees and ocean. An inclination of the head to the right or left reveals some pretty dire twentieth-century housing, but this is in part masked by mature trees. Only a row of swanked-up houses to the north really intrudes on the view and causes me to curse the previous lessees, who might, with a little imagination, have weighted down a branch of the mighty fig to the left of the house to provide horizontal obliteration.

Writing about Bronte House in the *Sydney Morning Herald* in November 1924, one Martyn Threlfall noted that 'the hand of the builder has been busy' in the surrounding areas. 'Red bricks and red tiles and the spacious verandahs of the American bungalows now surround the old-world charm of the Bronte Estate.' Earlier, in the 1880s, an unidentified writer contrasted the quaint picturesqueness of Bronte House with 'the snug stuccoed parvenu genteel villas which are springing up all round us and blotting the beauty of the surrounding scenery with their prim white newness and bare formal terraced grounds'. But the reality is that house and garden remain relatively secluded.

I can remember that first morning I walked through the gate to take tea

BELOW TOP: A Victorian needlework cushion.

BELOW BOTTOM: Regency candlesticks and a Victorian skeleton clock.

OPPOSITE TOP LEFT: A view of the Isle of Skye and Cuillin Hills, by John Glover, hangs over my bookshelves in the drawing room. The 1845 'Gothick' wallpaper was reprinted by hand in England from original wooden blocks.

OPPOSITE TOP RIGHT: A view of the present-day dining room. The books are removed for dinner parties and chairs drawn up to the table.

OPPOSITE BOTTOM LEFT: The early-nineteenth-century lamps on the chimneypiece in the drawing room were designed by Porden. They flank a clock in the Troubadour Gothic taste.

OPPOSITE BOTTOM RIGHT: Grand Tour souvenirs deployed in the dining room.

the garden at Bronte

with Selmes; I was enchanted. The house sat as trim on its site as a neat little frigate at its mooring. I walked in through the rooms which, even with wet plaster and lifted floorboards, were as seductive as they remain, and out onto the tessellated tile verandah overlooking a broad sweeping lawn and trees and eventually that same sun and sea I travelled from Summer Hill to enjoy decades before.

That first visit left me with the overwhelming feeling that this was the house in which I wanted to live and a garden I desperately needed to rescue from neglect. From that moment on, I fantasised about what I might do if ever I was lucky enough to live there. I replanned the garden in my head. Even with its potential unrealised, the place was magical. How might it look with planting that merged its then-isolated garden with that of the park beyond, rather than denying its existence in a doomed search for seclusion? I thought of the trees I might plant, the way the borders might be better organised and, most of all, how this adorable house and its garden might be made all of apiece, not simply a dwelling shrouded from public view by masses of undifferentiated green.

decline and fall

The Selmes occupancy was a short one, a mere two years and six months. He moved back to England, bought Lygrove, near Avon, Gloucestershire, a superb estate complete with a late-fifteenth-century manor house, which he crammed with more antiques and pictures. Ever restless, bored with Lygrove, he bought yet another house. That was in 1988, but before he could move in, he died.

Prior to leaving Sydney for the last time, Selmes telephoned me with an offer to sell me the lease. Although we had not spoken for some time, he was not one to let a small matter of a ruptured friendship get in the way of a deal. I was sorely tempted but was going through a marriage break-up at the time and, despite my passionate desire to live there, had other things on my mind besides assuming responsibility for an historic house and its garden. Politely declining his offer, I recommended to him a real estate agent, the colourful Billy Bridges. He had clients who had recently sold an important colonial house near Goulburn and were looking for somewhere to live in Sydney. Billy took them to see Bronte House and, like everyone who claps eyes on the place, they fell in love with it and snapped it up.

In many ways the next nine years were to prove an unhappy period for this house. Selmes had cut corners on the repair of the house and upkeep appeared to be a low priority for the new tenants. The neglect began to tell. One heard tales of the dodgy condition of the roof. Slates skedaddled all over the place. Leaks proliferated. Given

OPPOSITE: In the small entrance foyer, a French Empire ormolu clock shows a gardener with bucket, spade and rake.

ABOVE: Lucifer, the inherited cat.

OVERLEAF: I was unaware that these metal rockers were known as 'digestive chairs' until the noted English gardener Sir Roy Strong and his wife visited. Lady Strong told me they were used for sitting in after a heavy meal so that the gentle rocking would aid digestion. The original was made by R. W. Winfield and Co. of Birmingham in 1851. The simplicity of the design and its practicality ensured that the chair remained in production by Winfield well into the twentieth century.

low or no maintenance, the building and garden fell into obvious and serious disrepair. Downpipes resembled string bags: scraps of metal held together with filaments of rust. As for the garden, it was, frankly, a mess.

Alarmed at the lack of maintenance, the obvious decay, apparent even to the casual passer-by, and the failure of the lessee to comply with requirements that the house be opened to the public for the designated six days a year, Waverley Council, in 1992, commissioned a condition report from Clive Lucas. On 10 June 1992 he submitted a list of eleven items needing urgent attention. These ranged from termite infestation to re-pointing of the external walls. Council then called for a second, fuller report from the well-known conservation architect Howard Tanner, a local resident. He submitted it in July 1992. It made depressing reading.

Tanner summed up the situation in the concluding paragraph of his report:

> Bronte House is an important colonial cottage. Externally, while the ground and joinery have generally been satisfactorily maintained, the public impression of the house is one of shabbiness, of failing wall joints and lime wash finishes, of missing roof slates and corroded roof gutters and downpipes. Internally the condition of the house is more satisfactory, although damp in various forms is evident in scattered locations throughout. The house now requires a programme of external repairs and maintenance and it is recommended that these works be undertaken during 1992 to preclude further deterioration.

By that time the tenants' marriage had suffered a parallel decline. They separated, with the wife staying on in the mouldering house. Tanner's report had finally shaken the Council into action and, early in 1993, an order to undertake extensive repairs was served on the tenant. Despite their separation, the lease on Bronte House was

It must be painful for Roberts's heirs and successors to imagine what those 200 acres might be worth today! No more grants were made until 1827, and in the next five years only a further seven.

Colonial grandees and new rich preferred views over the tranquil waters of Sydney Harbour to those of the wild Pacific Ocean and chose their land accordingly, but Mortimer Lewis had a more original eye than most of his fellow settlers. In January 1836 he purchased 12 acres at Nelson Bay. In his short time in the colony, Lewis must have quickly cottoned on to the advantage of a cool breeze off the sea in the searing heat of a Sydney February, for this initial purchase of land included the site of the present house, high above and with a commanding view of the ocean.

Over the following two years, Lewis greatly increased his holdings at Nelson Bay, assembling a magnificent spread of 42 acres that included the valley to the west of the house, complete with freshwater creek and waterfall, part of the headland to the north, and all of the headland to the south. Included in the parcel was all of Bronte Beach.

With an architect's eye for siting, he chose a magnificent position for the house into which he and his wife proposed to move: an elevated plateau at the head of the valley, sheltered to the south by a fine sandstone cliff and protected to the north as well. In what was to become an Australian rite, he designed his dream home and proceeded to lay the foundations. Roads were cut and the property fenced. A slab hut was probably constructed at about this time and a home farm established. Then, in 1842, financial crisis brought ruin to many in the fledgling colony, including Lewis, and work was abruptly halted. The house remained unfinished for three years.

Just what kind of a house Lewis intended to build is uncertain. The plans mentioned in the *Australian Town and Country Journal* have not survived, or if they have, remain unidentified. It was probably, as the architectural historian Dr James Broadbent has suggested, inspired by a design published in J. J. Ricauti's *Rustic Architecture*. Sir Thomas Mitchell was a friend of Lewis's, and he had a copy of this book in his library, so it is reasonable to assume an influence. The four-square plan of the house has a simplicity characteristic of Lewis's other work, and his hallmark details of bay and bow windows are also incorporated.

But Mitchell may have loaned Lewis another book: *The Royal Lodges in Windsor Great Park* by H. B. Ziegler. For Broadbent, the design for Bronte House is 'unmistakably' taken from a design for the Keeper's Lodge on the Windsor Road, a building tricked out with a romantic turret of which there were to be four in Bronte House when completed. This hypothesis would tally with the report in the *Australian Town and Country Journal* that Lewis intended to construct a 'baronial-style' residence.

It is tantalising to speculate about how the house might have looked if finished by Lewis and not by others. It may have resembled the Keeper's Lodge at Windsor,

ABOVE TOP: A miniature portrait of Mortimer Lewis, the first owner of the Bronte estate, painted before he and his wife left London in 1830.

ABOVE BOTTOM: A miniature of Mortimer's wife, Elizabeth.

OPPOSITE: A watercolour by Georgiana Lowe with a view of Bronte Beach and the cliffs at the southern end, circa 1845. Bronte House is visible on the hill with its farm to the north, close to the beach. When the Lowes bought the house it was only partially completed. It was finished to accord with Mrs Lowe's Romantic taste.

or Richmond Villa, the neo-Gothic house he designed and built for himself and his family in 1849 when business eventually picked up. Originally overlooking the Domain, the villa was dismantled in 1975 and re-erected in Kent Street and now serves as headquarters for the Society of Australian Genealogists. That particular house has a number of features that are pre-echoed at Bronte: bold bay windows, stripped-down Gothic details such as glazing bars contrived as inverted 'V's; but it is plainer and more consistent in style. And it is a two-storey building, which may have been the intention at Nelson Bay, to maximise the advantages of ocean views and sea breezes.

Speculation, while fascinating, is really irrelevant. In 1838 Lewis refused an excellent offer only to see it sold later to Robert and Georgiana Lowe for a fraction of the earlier offer. It was the Lowes who finished the place and imbued the house and its garden with much of the magic it retains to this day.

the Lowes

We have bought a little estate of forty-two acres, four miles from Sydney, on the sea; it is lovely beyond conception. We have given only £420 for it; it is fenced – and the foundation of the house laid and roads cut – the value of the improvements about £200. We are finishing the house. It was sold by an unfortunate mortgagee in England, put up to public auction, and by a lucky chance fell to us; £4,000 was refused for the land four years ago. I shall make some drawings of the views. The scenery resembles Jersey, but is far more beautiful – the vegetation is so lovely. We have a beautiful bay to ourselves – I may say it is our own – the trees line the shore with drives through them. We have a waterfall of sixty feet, and this runs through a fine valley. It is a most romantic spot and just suits my tastes.

Georgiana Lowe in a letter to England, 1845

'Bronte House' is far too grand a name for this building, a relic of late-nineteenth-century nomenclatural aggrandisement. For Robert and Georgiana Lowe, it was a cottage, albeit of the fancier kind known as a *cottage orné*, the fashionable Regency description for a picturesque folly or rural retreat.

Mortimer Lewis may have inclined towards a baronial-style building, but the Lowes had fewer pretensions and a less assured income. Besides, they never intended to settle permanently in New South Wales, and although, after they left in 1845, both wrote and spoke enthusiastically about their time at Nelson Bay, they never returned.

They must have made a curious couple: he a brilliant orator, able to dash off a poem in Latin or Greek in a trice and with a phenomenal memory; she, while far from being his intellectual equal, lively, plucky, artistically inclined, capable and thrifty. Their combined breeding and education instantly placed the Lowes at the sparsely populated summit of contemporary colonial society.

Physically they were distinctive, too. Mrs Lowe was masculine in manner and appearance, while her husband was tall, thin and an albino, as was his eldest sister, who, in Lowe's words, was 'very keenly alive to this misfortune'. And his eyesight was appalling. 'The peculiarity of my eyes,' he wrote, 'consists in the total absence of colouring matter. This, with fair complexion and snow white hair, gives an impression, in a man, of effeminacy.'

Bobby Lowe, as he was often impertinently dubbed, had more to worry about than the negative impression his pallor might make on the public, or the colour – or

absence thereof – of his eyes. His greatest fear was that he might become blind, and that concern was one of the reasons for the decision to come to Australia. 'Because the eyes are impatient of light,' he wrote of his condition, 'the eyelids must always nearly be closed and so I have never been able to enjoy the luxury of staring anyone full in the face.' Confirmation of this acute optical sensitivity lingers at Bronte House in the form of a system, unique in colonial houses, of light-excluding shutters in the bay window of the dining room, where he probably did most of his reading.

Robert Lowe was born in 1811 at Bingham in Nottingham, the son of a clergyman. Educated at Winchester School, he graduated from Oxford in 1833, and a year later he was elected a fellow of Magdalen College, earning additional money as a private tutor. He was called to the Bar at Lincoln's Inn in 1842.

In 1835, despite strong parental opposition, he had married the high-spirited Miss Georgiana Orred, the second of four daughters of a prosperous Cheshire family. By 1842 Lowe's eyesight was worsening and his doctors in England recommended an outdoor life. He might have retired to rural quiet, but instead he and Georgiana boarded the *Aden* and set sail for Sydney, arriving on 2 October. He was thirty-one.

The year 1842 had not been a good one for the colony: an economic crisis meant financial ruin for many people. The *Sydney Morning Herald* of January the following year sounded a note of retrospective gloom: 'the year 1842 would long be remembered as one of the darkest in the history of New South Wales.'

Because his family had produced many ministers of religion, a career for which he was also thought eminently suitable but rejected, Lowe brought with him letters of introduction to Bishop Broughton, the recently appointed first Bishop of the Church of England in Australia, one of the chief figures of influence in the colony. His wife had somewhat grander connections, being a distant relative of the Governor, Sir George Gipps, and, for a short period after their arrival, the Lowes were guests of the Governor and his Lady at Government House, Parramatta, the vice-regal couple's country residence.

After their stay at Parramatta, the Lowes returned to Sydney, where they took lodgings until the house they had chosen for their home was prepared. This house still stands, one of the two remaining components of Horbury Terrace in Macquarie Street, opposite the State Library of New South Wales, and close to what Robert Lowe described as 'the beautiful salt lake, as we should call it in England, which forms the peerless Harbour which will, I believe, always place Sydney at the head of the Australian colonies'.

Lowe was a tetchy character, 'the most quarrelsome man in the New World' according to what might now be called a profile, complete with caricature, published in the English magazine *Vanity Fair* on 27 February 1869. Quickly admitted to the local Bar, he was then appointed to the Legislative Council of New South Wales by Governor

OPPOSITE TOP: A view of the western side of the house.

OPPOSITE BOTTOM: A pair of Staffordshire jugs depicting Lord Nelson, after whom Nelson Bay was named, which later become Bronte.

ABOVE LEFT: This watercolour by Georgiana Lowe clearly shows the beginnings of her garden, circa 1845.

ABOVE RIGHT: A watercolour *en grisaille* of the eastern side of Bronte House by an anonymous artist in the late-nineteenth century.

Gipps, with whom he soon fell out and resigned the appointment. He then stood for election and was voted into the same Council as a representative of the squatters, with whom he also disagreed. At the subsequent election, he was returned as the Member for Sydney as a representative of the working class. Securely installed in Parliament, he then refused to support his new constituents' efforts to relieve unemployment. He was twice challenged to a duel with pistols, and sabotaged Wentworth's first attempt to establish Sydney University on the grounds that a close friend and political ally with whom he had also fallen out was to be one of the proposed senators.

Clearly his great talents were matched by an inability to sustain any kind of friendship, especially with those whom he saw as his social or intellectual inferiors. Back in Britain, this flaw in his character, combined with a disapproval of Queen Victoria, with whom he quarrelled publicly in 1876 over her desire to be declared Empress of India, put paid to his ambitions to succeed Gladstone as the leader of the Liberal Party and possibly as Prime Minister. In the event, he had to settle for a viscountcy and the Queen even disapproved of that honour, observing that a baronetcy would be 'ample' and any higher order 'objectionable'.

Georgiana Lowe seems to have been an altogether more agreeable soul, although she was described by former servants, after she had returned to England and was out of earshot, as 'haughty'. As far as her fellow colonists were concerned, she was a roaring snob, but she had many mitigating accomplishments. She 'could fell a tree with any man, could fence in an allotment, and was a good hand with the saw'. She was also a 'capital rider' and liked nothing better than to take to the bush on horseback, scouring the

countryside, riding along New South Head Road – then under construction – and often riding out to meet her husband and returning with him in the evenings. On more than one occasion she rode with him along the coast from Wollongong back to Nelson Bay. Her sudden appearance, tearing out of the bush at full tilt, dressed in her dark riding habit, earned her among the startled settlers along the way the sobriquet 'The Black Angel'.

It was not, however, all smooth riding. In one of her numerous letters to relatives, she wrote:

> I have been most unfortunate lately: a few days ago my horse threw me. I had a knapsack into which I put flowers, curiosities, &c, it fell from my saddle, startled the horse, and I fell also, with my face to the ground, and cut my lip open and bruised my cheekbone badly. I sent for a surgeon, who sewed up my lip, put leeches on my temple, and I am now pretty well again and have very little pain left.

OPPOSITE: Few gardeners recorded their efforts and the environment in which they were making their garden as comprehensively as did Georgiana Lowe. Some eighteen of her accomplished watercolours record the house, its setting, details of the building, the coastline and some of the plants, native and introduced, in her garden.

TOP LEFT: The waterfall that cascaded over rocks into a stream that flowed into the sea. The waterfall survives but the stream is now a stormwater channel.

TOP RIGHT: The giant bamboo (*Bambusa balcooa*) planted and painted by Georgiana Lowe still survives in the garden at Bronte.

BOTTOM LEFT: One of the few plants known to have been grown at Bronte in the 1840s by Georgiana Lowe is the banana. These trees survive today.

BOTTOM RIGHT: A *Xanthorrhoea australis*, often known as a 'blackboy', and so called because of its fire-blackened trunk. This Australian native must have been part of the original vegetation in the gully near Bronte House.

Georgiana's 'masculine accomplishments' went hand in hand with more genteel ones. She sketched very well indeed. Her watercolours are extremely well done. Fine watercolours and drawings of her Antipodean home from every angle and of the adjacent coastline, as well as sketches of native flora and topographical views of the Illawarra, flowed from her brush and pencil. She was also an 'excellent pen-woman', an exemplary correspondent whose passion for letter-writing, allied with her skills as an artist, combined to create a lively record of the Lowe occupancy, even though they lived in the house they built for fewer than five years.

But, above all, Georgiana was a serious gardener: digging, weeding, directing, soliciting seeds and plants, collecting specimens of native plants and generally busying herself in the garden. Her enthusiasm for horticulture is evident from another of those letters to relatives in England:

> My time now passes much to my taste. I am in my garden all day & quite delight in cultivating our place. My brother John has sent me a large collection for the new annuals & vegetables. I shall have great pleasure in watching them. I have just been planting seeds that were collected on Dr Leichardt's [sic] expedition – a gentleman who accompanied him gave me a few seeds of each new flower they discovered.

Much as she loved her garden, Georgiana abandoned it willingly. On 27 January 1850 she and Robert set sail for England aboard the *Kate*, accompanied by their two adopted children, orphans of a widow whose murderer Robert had defended in a sensational

criminal case. But, even now, it is Georgiana's spirit that pervades the place rather than that of her brilliant husband.

In one letter home, Georgiana inveighed against the local population:

> Our emigrants are a most worthless & indolent race. They are idle, dirty, insolent, & dishonest, & their ignorance of all that is useful is beyond all idea. We have the lowest & worst of the Irish Catholic population & they are I think the most degraded race of people that Europe can produce. Their only aim seems to be to gain a few shillings to get drunk with. They have no gratitude for kindness & I believe their miserable cowardice is their reason for not committing any crime however terrible. We have a few good female servants from the North of Ireland & these are really valuable. I am highly impressed with the different class the North & South of Ireland contain.

What would Georgiana think of the present occupant? When dabbling in a little amateur genealogy, I came across the name of one of my forebears from County Limerick. At about the time the Lowes were moving into their charming cottage, he was less salubriously accommodated. In official records his address is given simply as 'The Jail, Sydney'.

the garden at Bronte

an imagined garden

You can form no idea of the beauty of this climate: our winters are delicious;
the finest October day you can recall to mind is only a faint resemblance of the
weather here. I fear I shall look with horror on the leafless trees when I return
home; all the flowers are splendid. The only fault is, they are all on bushes,
so the ground is never coloured by them.

Georgiana Lowe in a letter to England, 1845

Just what sort of a garden Georgiana Lowe made, or what flowers she grew there during
those full and delightful days she spent working in it, is unclear. In one of her drawings
we can see a generalised shrub or two and an unidentifiable curlicue of vine threaded
through the trefoil frets of a verandah post. She painted a specimen of *Xanthorrhoea
australis*, known as the 'blackboy' or 'grass tree' (see page 30) – an unusual native plant

OPPOSITE: Some idea of the sparse
vegetation around the house in
1845 can be gleaned from this lovely
watercolour by Georgiana Lowe,
showing the octagonal turret at the
north-eastern corner.

RIGHT: A drawing by a member of
the King family showing a young girl,
possibly Annie Macarthur, seated in
the garden of Vineyard, the house at
Rydalmere built by her father, Hannibal,
in 1835. The simple rustic fence
provided the inspiration for the one
at Bronte.

that must have had singular appeal for her – and she made a beautiful drawing of the giant bamboo (*Bambusa balcooa*) still flourishing in the garden (see page 30). Given that she and Robert were regular visitors to Government House in Sydney, it is probable that this derived from the one still growing in the grounds of the vice-regal residence.

Georgiana was an avid collector of seeds and plants, and it's almost certain that her garden contained native species as well as the shrubs and cottage annuals grown from the seeds her brother sent her from England. It's tempting to think she planted the Port Jackson fig (*Ficus rubiginosa*) that sits majestically atop a rocky outcrop on the north-east side of the garden, and even more tempting to imagine that the rare podocarpus growing alongside was nurtured from one of those seeds from Leichhardt's expedition.

But no actual plan of her garden survives, nor any drawing that would serve as a basis for a speculative 'recreation'. All we have are the ecstatic written descriptions larded through her letters ('All our improvements have been answered and our garden is not only a productive one but most picturesque'); a single mention of a specific plant ('I wish I could show you my bananas and the fruit you would not despise'); and frequent reference to the satisfaction it gave her ('I now feel the value of my love for nature').

What does survive, however, is a fine lithograph map of the property, then 57 acres in all, made in 1861 for the auctioneers Richardson & Wrench, who, in that year, put the property up for sale as fifteen lots. By this time, the name 'Bronte' had been attached to the estate and 'Bronte House' to the central building.

This map, prepared by Reuss & Browne, a firm of Sydney surveyors, shows specific areas designated for cultivation, areas to the west of the house for a kitchen garden, orchard and vineyard, and a further kitchen garden situated between the house and the beach.

The Lowes had been unable to divest themselves of their property before they left Australia in 1850. They ultimately did and during the subsequent decade it changed hands a number of times. It is reasonable to hypothesise that none of these short-term owners made any radical alterations to grounds or house, so this plan probably shows the garden much as the Lowes left it.

Accompanying the map are several descriptions of the garden:

The pleasure grounds include lawn, flower gardens, wild shrubberies, hotbeds &c, all well arranged, and planted with valuable shrubs and flowering plants, in the best style of landscape gardening. They extend to the rivulet, and are intersected with gravel walks and shady avenues, overshadowed with evergreens, leading to a wide-spreading sandy beach, washed by the dark blue waters of the Pacific.

OPPOSITE: A rare semicircular Regency wrought-iron garden seat, acquired from the estate of the noted London hostess Lady 'Bubbles' Rothermere, tucks neatly into a shaped bank of herbaceous plants at the southern end of the Eastern Terrace.

ABOVE TOP: One of David Austin's most beautiful roses, *Rosa* 'Abraham Darby'.

ABOVE BOTTOM: *Rosa* 'Windrush'.

Georgiana's 1840s watercolours show the landscape surrounding the house to be thinly vegetated (see pages 29 and 32). In the decade and more between the time of their departure and the penning of this description, some of the trees she planted had clearly grown substantially.

Lot 2 of the subdivision carries a further example of real estate prose in a somewhat baroque description of the gardens, but again it is unspecific as to plants. There was 'a beautiful grass lawn' and the 'residue of the grounds are laid out in terraces – the natural advantages of the romantic position being improved by the talent and taste of the landscape gardener. Each terrace is laid out into flower beds intersected with gravel walks, and is traversed by two never-failing rivulets. The plants and shrubs are of the most choice and rare description, having been procured at a great cost; the whole forming one of the finest botanical collections of the sort in the colony.' While still maddeningly vague on the precise types of choice and rare plants and shrubs, one does have a hint here that this was no ordinary garden and, in refashioning it, I have tried to assemble unusual rather than routine nursery material.

Further descriptions of the garden later in the nineteenth century are contained in an even more purple text produced by the auctioneers Watkin & Watkin, who, in 1892, were appointed to handle the subdivision of the property on behalf of the prosperous Sydney ironmonger J. B. Holdsworth, the 1861 purchaser of the house and garden, and a man whose name survives embossed on the door of the cast-iron fuel stove in the old kitchen and in a cruder, less commercial form, scratched childishly onto a glass window in what is now the laundry.

The Watkin & Watkin booklet is a lavish affair (see pages 42 and 43), with original sepia photographs of the garden and house tipped in by hand, and flamboyant, descriptive language. Byron, Tennyson, Verdi, Theocritus, Jansen Tasman, Deniehy, Demosthenes, Cicero, Calypso, Aphrodite, Odysseus and Lord Nelson are all invoked or quoted in an extended paean to the various attractions of the estate – attractions that, ironically, would have vanished entirely had the subdivision of the by-then 77 acres proceeded in its advertised form.

Noted in this rhapsodic description of 'woodland and sylvan sites, not to be equalled in any English nobleman's park' are 'The Waterfall', 'The Glen', 'The Rosery' and 'The Lovers' Walk', all shown in photographs from which one can identify a number of individual plants. Once more one reads of 'grounds and gardens ornamentally laid out and planted with tropical ferns and luxuriantly and richly timbered', of 'a ravine where the spectator may well imagine himself in some distant valley, amid the mountains far away from human habitation', and of the 'enchanting view of the sea over the tops and through a vista of pine trees and shrubs', a view that still survives, albeit in a somewhat more diminished form due to a century's worth of growth of those pines.

OPPOSITE: Five types of bananas now grow at Bronte: the ornamental *Musa ornata* and *M. velutina* (pictured), both with spectacular pink fruit; the giant-leafed *M. ensete*; *M. zebrina*, with large, flag-like leaves striped in khaki; and *M. acuminata* 'Dwarf Cavendish'. In 2001 the last produced two magnificent clumps of bananas, which gardener Myles Baldwin cut off and hung from the verandah posts to ripen. Of excellent flavour, they inspired a flurry of banana cakes, banana smoothies and banana pancakes, and many were given away to friends and visitors.

In the photograph, the 'Rosery' looks somewhat shambolic and it is impossible to identify any of the varieties grown, but we do know that Mrs Lowe, in another of those chatty letters to relatives, wrote, 'Unless you could see them you would not believe how beautiful the roses are here.' She had been visiting Elizabeth Bay House, home of Alexander Macleay, a careful recorder of his garden plantings from 1830, and he listed thirty-four roses in his garden: five Gallica, four Alba, six Damask, six Centifolia, one Moss, two China ('Hume's Blush' and 'Parks' Yellow'), three Noisette and seven others. No doubt the persuasive Mrs Lowe coaxed cuttings of some of these from Mr Macleay.

We also know that, at the close of the nineteenth century, weeping willows grew on the property, that there were hothouses, an orchard, a vinery and a fernery. We learn too that there was a roomy and convenient gardener's cottage, but again, there is a maddening absence of specificity.

Georgiana's drawings and a variety of late-nineteenth-century photographs show a virtual wilderness from which were carved designated garden areas, but thirty years into the next century, the place appears quite shorn of any immediate garden. A photograph published in the *Sydney Morning Herald* of 26 July 1935, which accompanied the one on the opposite page, shows the then premier, Sir Bertram Stevens, inspecting the 'historic Bronte House, Bronte, which the Government has been asked to purchase for the people'.

ABOVE: Both verandahs on the western front of the house were enclosed in the later nineteenth century, one with several courses of sandstone block to make a kind of conservatory, later glassed over, and the other with lattice.

OPPOSITE: Preserve or demolish and develop – the future of Bronte House was debated for almost fifty years. In 1935 the then Premier Sir Bertram Stevens (right) and his wife, seen here descending to the Eastern Terrace with then owner Austin Ebsworth (left of Mrs Stevens) and another un-identified man, were shown over the property in an attempt to persuade the State government to acquire the property.

the garden at Bronte

The lawn runs right up, slap-bang to the eastern side of the house and, apart from some kind of clinging vine on the octagonal turret and another unidentifiable vine clambering up between the bay window and the verandah, there is no sign of a garden apart from a patch of wiry lawn. Indeed, this space adjacent to the octagonal turret is occupied solely by a rather large corrugated-iron water tank.

Many English gardens, great and small, have retained their original form for centuries. Even if they haven't, aerial photographs now enable garden archaeologists to recreate an authentic form, but given the changes at Bronte – changes that range from the interpolation of a main road, to subdivision of the grounds and both public and institutional use of the house – it was clear from the outset that any reconstruction of the garden was bound to be speculative. In other words, this would be an imagined garden, appropriate to the house and with some 'period' plants, but needing less man-power than Mrs Lowe had available to her when she laid it out. And rehabilitation, regeneration, restoration, call it what you will, would have to rely on a pathetic handful of hints thrown out in general descriptions of the property from sales catalogues. The only plants anyone could claim with any certainty to have survived from or to have grown here in the 1840s are bananas, bamboo, Gymea lily (*Doryanthes excelsa*) and various regional pines. To this list can be added assorted anonymous ferns, willows and roses.

In a fascinating interview given to Sydney's *Sunday Sun*, and published on 13 November 1938, the Australian poet Dame Mary Gilmore recalled that her grandfather, Hugh Beattie, who had been the Lowes's bailiff, planted waratahs here – the first to be successfully grown in a Sydney garden. Dame Mary saw them still flourishing in the late 1890s along with the remnants of 'a maze' her grandfather had made for Mrs Lowe.

But while lacking detailed evidence of specific planting, I did have to hand good modern proposals in the form of two late-twentieth-century plans from which ideas could be drawn. The first of these had been devised by Dr (then plain James) Broadbent. Dated April 1983, it had been only partially implemented.

A replacement Norfolk Island pine, identical to the one Georgiana had sketched, had been planted in the centre of the circular lawn and is now a noble and handsome specimen, soaring some 60 metres skywards. Also planted, and still flourishing, were a *Magnolia grandiflora* in the bed at the end of the southern shrubbery and a pair of *Viburnum tinus* flanking the steps in this area.

Other remnants of the partially executed Broadbent plan remained in the form of two sad and straggly lilly pillys (*Acmena smithii*). In his eagerness for privacy, Selmes had become impatient with the slow growth of a line of seven lilly pillys he had planted along the southern fence of the property, and had replaced them with fast-growing Hill's weeping figs (*Ficus microcarpa* var. *hillii*).

At the edge of the Eastern Terrace, overlooking park and ocean, where, in the late-nineteenth century a buttressed wall of sandstone blocks had been built to create a level lawn beyond which the land falls away steeply to the rockery, Broadbent had indicated a simple, low fence over which was to scramble a variety of creepers – lantana, passionfruit, jasmine and snail vine. In proposing this, he was influenced by a sketch of a similar fence from an album made by a member of the King family (see page 33). The rustic fence was an accepted solution to the problem of demarcating cultivated and uncultivated sections of a landscape while allowing it to appear unified.

But between Broadbent's dream and the reality, fell the shadow of compromise. He had wanted a light, decorative structure similar to the Macarthur model, made of crisscrossed twigs laced together with twine. What was eventually installed was an arrangement of thick posts with chicken-coop wire, and by the time I moved in the whole lot – passionfruit, jasmine and snail vine – had collapsed under a wave of rampant lantana.

At regular intervals through the northern borders, Broadbent had placed old camellias of unspecified variety and it's certain that these would have been historically correct. But the problem with historical rectitude is that it's often horticulturally untenable. Though far from mature, these old-variety camellias had already begun to obscure sun from large areas of the borders. Some of the planting Broadbent envisaged for the borders was hanging in, but, on the whole, remnants of this intelligent but challenging

OPPOSITE: One of the three specimens of Bull Bay magnolia (*M. grandiflora* 'Exmouth') I planted along the southern boundary fence. Bought as a five-year-old specimen, it streaked away and was subsequently clipped into a conical shape.

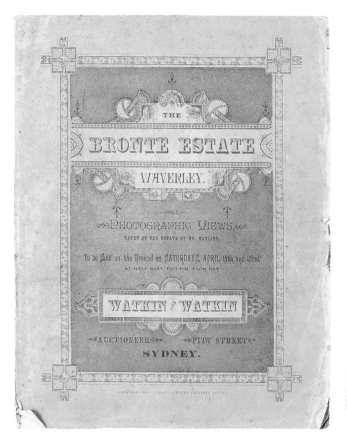

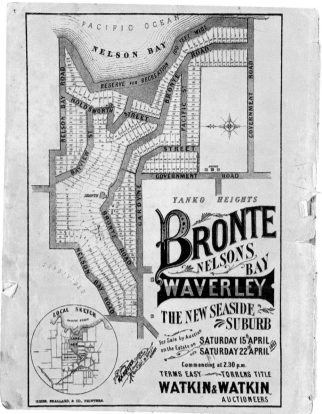

scheme were few and far between. When I moved in I found a copy of his plan. It might have been wonderful if – and it's a big 'if' – it had been fully and faithfully implemented and consistently maintained. Using it, however, it was possible to pinpoint the material that had survived – the old-fashioned camellias, the magnolia planted near the street, some Dutch irises, and lots of dietes, a plant so tough that it would probably flourish in cement.

Further Broadbent suggestions had included a big hibiscus at the northern end of the front lawn, a circular bed at the other end in the High Victorian Gardenesque taste with a century plant (*Agave americana* var. *mediopicta*) surrounded by red gladioli, geraniums and waves of watsonias planted through the grass. These suggestions appear never to have been carried out.

Some of what was selectively implemented had dire consequences. A bed stuffed with pale-blue-flowered common plumbago turned out to be infected with phytophthora, which was subsequently to become a sore trial. Most soft-wooded plants harbour this soil-borne native virus and it dispatched, in short order, numerous apple blossom hibiscus, a couple of echiums and some roses before I began to plant hardier material.

the garden at Bronte

OPPOSITE LEFT: The cover of the brochure prepared by real estate auctioneers Watkin & Watkin for a proposed 1882 subdivision of the property.

OPPOSITE RIGHT: What might have been. The proposed carve-up left Bronte House marooned in the middle of a suburban sprawl, without views or curtilage.

BELOW: Frontispiece and pages from the Watkin & Watkin brochure promoting the 'GREAT SEASIDE EASTER SALE'. Copies of this brochure, expensively produced with specially commissioned photographs pasted in, are extremely rare and only a few have survived. This one was given to me by English descendants of the Ebsworth family.

OVERLEAF: The garden takes shape as a tangle of roses and honeysuckle smother an arched trellis, and succulents and flaxes – miniscule when planted – reach mature size.

When the last lessees moved in they were clearly unhappy with Broadbent's strict historical approach to the garden. They also may have needed to demonstrate to Waverley Council their commitment to house and garden, so in August 1985 they commissioned a second plan from Colin Smith, a skilled gardener and landscape designer. He delivered his drawings the following January and suggested sweeping changes.

To be introduced were a fern walk, a daisy garden, a rose garden and features such as a fountain and statuary. Apart from the allusions to the earlier fern walk and a rosary, Smith's was an almost anti-historicist approach, designed to create a spectacular new garden. As far as one can tell, no element of his scheme was ever implemented and Smith suspects that the plan was commissioned simply to persuade the Council that their new tenants were serious about the garden.

Now while both of these schemes were useful, I elected to go in a different direction. I wanted to make no radical changes to the basic form of the garden. Besides being inappropriate, fashionable flagging, neo-Tuscan box borders and hedges clipped to a madness are not to my taste. Nor were major earthworks, lap pools and other aids to gracious contemporary living. A short path was curved here, an arch introduced there, but, for the most part, the paths, beds and general layout as interpreted by Lucas and Broadbent were kept as they were.

So when I am asked, as I often am, the question, 'Is this the way it originally looked?' my reply is always the same. 'A garden is a growing thing. This is how it has grown.'

But the truth is that it is a garden of the imagination, filled with the sorts of things Mrs Lowe might have planted had she had access to them.

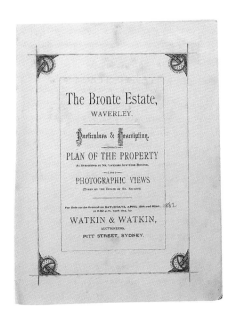

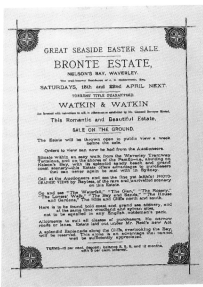

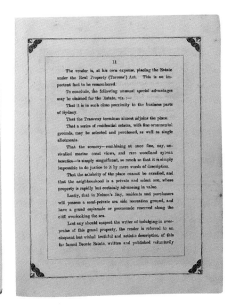

experiment and elimination

Vita Sackville-West, who created an internationally renowned

garden at Sissinghurst, in England, once observed that she was

not running an intensive care ward for ailing plants. Nor am I.

If a plant doesn't want to grow here, no matter how desirable or

historically appropriate it is, it comes out, replaced by something

that finds conditions more congenial.

let there be light

Shade is the enemy of all old gardens. When a garden is first laid out or improved, trees are inevitably involved: a specimen tree in a prominent place; a clump of trees for privacy; one or more favourite flowering trees. Usually they are planted as wand-like saplings, but trees have a habit of growing and some grow very big indeed. This seems to be a fact that escapes many gardeners who shop for a tree at a nursery or garden centre and somehow imagine that it will always be as it was when purchased – neat, compact, attractive of shape and unnaturally healthy. As they mature, however, trees and large shrubs, like humans, change and alter the nature of the space they inhabit and the character and form of a garden. Sometimes this is no bad thing, but trees also cast shadows, and the repertoire of plants that will flourish in full or even partial shade is fairly limited, at least in climates akin to Sydney's.

So my very first task in this vast and rambling garden was to deal with the trees. There were too many of them, and too many were the dreaded camphor laurels. *Cinnamomum camphora* has been declared a noxious weed in some parts of Australia because of its rampant growth and gross feeding habit that leaves the surrounding soil exsanguinated. Handsome though they may be, and heady the smell emitted by leaves and cut branches, they are a pest, as anyone who has ever driven along the back roads of the beautiful far north coast of New South Wales knows. A few of these camphor laurels at Bronte would be retained, but many had to go to reduce the stygian gloom underneath and allow full or dappled sunlight into as many parts of the garden as possible.

Ditto with the camellias. Nothing would grow under them. Nor were they, to my way of thinking, particularly attractive. They were mostly *Camellia japonica* in chilly bluish reds with flowers that quickly browned and resembled pendant dog droppings. However, it was for a reason other than their mouldy appearance that they went. They were planted dead-centre in the middle of the beds, and their continuing presence would have dictated a fusty shrubbery look when what I wanted was a sense of depth and variety. Had they been planted towards the back of the beds, they might have been allowed to remain, but their ongoing presence inhibited the placement of further tall material in the background.

At the north side of the house grew two frangipanis, the common *Plumeria rubra*. Now this is a tree I love and to which I have dedicated much space later in this book (see A Flurry of Frangipanis, page 166) but, after much consideration, I reluctantly decided to dispense with one. It was too close to other large plants and, again, shaded a bed in which it was important to have something growing at ground level other than moss and weeds.

PAGE 46: Ranks of seedlings await planting.

PAGE 47: A seventeenth-century fountain mask, now mounted on a wall on the western side of the house.

OPPOSITE: The late-November, early-December show of mixed agapanthus and orange cosmos obligingly flowering concurrently at the edge of the lawn on the eastern side of the house.

a battleground in Bronte

The temptation when making or remaking a garden is to get on with the interesting bits such as choosing and placing plants. This is a bit like hanging wallpaper on drummy plaster or laying carpet before repairing a leaky roof. Readying a garden for planting is the dullest, hardest and least rewarding of tasks. At Bronte the grind, disruption and cost of arboreal work was followed by equally daunting, depressing and expensive work to prepare for the fun part of gardening: the actual deployment of plants.

Early in 1995 we entered the second stage of reclamation of the garden, called, after the conflict current at the time, 'The Bosnian Period'. Politically incorrect, of course, and probably selfish, too, making an analogy between personal disruption and the upheaval of an entire country, but at times the scene both at house level and below, in the semitropical area, resembled landscapes made familiar to us by the extensive television coverage of successive crises in the Balkans. We were terrified that locals, long denied access, ergo unaware of the overgrown condition of the garden and the need for savage cutting-back, might complain that we were removing too much. A nosey passer-by had already telephoned the Council to air her distress about professional pruning of the giant bamboo (*Bambusa balcooa*) at the bottom of the garden, an early and urgent action as it was advancing steadily but surely in the direction of the Pacific Ocean.

We kept chainsaw activity to a minimum, often laboriously sawing off rotted trunks and superfluous limbs by hand so as not to attract attention. It had to be done, and although we were not carrying out any work unsanctioned by the appropriate local government authority and the Heritage Council, stealth seemed the most prudent course of action.

It is difficult to explain to the horticulturally challenged that it is not good practice to plant two potentially large trees within 3 metres of each other. Ultimately, one, and possibly both, will have to go, as happened to a handsome jacaranda and a *Tibouchina grandiflora* planted cheek by jowl as small trees by one of the entrance gates and growing locked in deadly competition for sun and space. Up to about 2 metres, their underpruned trunks grew straight and proud, but as soon as they reached the top of the fence and had space to spread, they decided to go their separate ways, splaying out at wild angles from each other. I would like to have saved both but it was not possible to save either and they fell to the saw, a double waste of good growing time. No-one likes to see any tree cut down (although I don't mind seeing any number of camphor laurels and Cocos palms bite the dust), but it did seem a pity to have to fell two trees, the flowers of which worked perfectly with the colour scheme subsequently implemented.

ABOVE: Most plants at Bronte House are raised from seed.

OPPOSITE: Bare bones. Only the clamshell under the tap to the right has remained the same size, in these beds which I call the White and Yellow Borders. All else is now a wanton flush of green and flowers.

the garden at Bronte

I had to keep reminding myself that I was not dealing with a *tabula rasa* here, starting from scratch with a nice open area in which one could do pretty much as one liked, planning and deploying plants as one might with a brand-new garden. No, what was under way was an attempt to shape and mould a collection of plant material that, although well established, had been allowed to become seriously shapeless, and we were doing so within the immutable parameters of brick borders and quirkily shaped beds.

There can be no denying that the garden as it existed when I moved in had a romantic, overgrown quality. It was full and green and not a square centimetre of soil could be seen. Nor could many of the surrounding houses. For the two previous lessees, privacy had been a kind of crusade. They had planted for instant isolation with no eye to either design or future form and not a lot of heed to creating the kind of garden the public might want to see. Romantic though this dense, impenetrable secret garden effect might have been, it was also blowsy and formless and it did not take long to realise that radical surgery was urgently needed, excisions essential.

Light, or lack thereof, was not our only problem. Parts of the border wore a gloomy municipal air. Originally the road leading to the house had terminated at the circular driveway, clearly shown in one of Georgiana Lowe's watercolours and in subsequent plans for the 1861 and 1882 subdivisions of the property. But when the road became a public thoroughfare, Bronte Road, and was pushed through to the beach, a section of the drive was sliced off, along with the pepper-pot tower at the south-eastern corner.

During the Selmes renovation the drive had been reconstructed and a new Norfolk Island pine planted in the centre as Mrs Lowe had done. That first pine still showed in photographs of the house in the latter part of the nineteenth century (see page 38), but during the period when the house had been used as a venue for weddings and parties, it had been removed and a ghastly cement fountain put in its place. The problem was that although the *illusion* of a circular drive was created by Selmes – and the lawn was, as it had always been, a perfect circle – the drive was incomplete, following the circumference of only about two-thirds of the central lawn. One drove in at a 'ten minutes to the hour' position and exited at 'twenty to'. At its narrowest section there was just a flowerbed less than a metre wide, and this meagre strip of dirt had been densely planted with blue agapanthus, a treatment that emphasised rather than disguised its narrowness. It was clear that the aggies would have to go, as would almost everything else popped in as an unconsidered space filler.

To avoid too obvious evidence of defoliation the northern border was tackled first. Everything here was removed. Everything. Right up to the moment of the first saw cut, I clung to the idea of keeping the odd plant, an old camellia or two, but if we were

OPPOSITE TOP LEFT: The compost bins, simple but effective.

OPPOSITE TOP RIGHT: Myles Baldwin gives a *Camellia sasanqua* its regular haircut.

OPPOSITE BOTTOM LEFT: Cannas on the up and up.

OPPOSITE BOTTOM RIGHT: Tools of the trade.

ABOVE: In autumn the garden is filled with benign spiders and their spun silvery webs.

ever to have anything growing here, more sun was needed, so the beds were virtually levelled. Not one blade of grass was left standing. It was as though some capricious blight had chosen to affect only this section of the garden.

This suburban equivalent of clear-felling revealed two major problems: onion weed and wretched soil. The onion weed was all carefully removed by hand. The gardener at the time, Brendan Lewis, had the same search-and-destroy attitude to this weed that Lord Mark had towards rabbits in *The Wings of the Dove*. Onion weed is insidious and if it gets a hold in a garden it can become a lifelong problem, soluble only by total soil replacement. Once rife throughout the garden at Bronte, it has now been virtually eliminated, and if it does appear it is seized upon as though it is a plant of the utmost rarity, although it is not treated as such. As a professional gardener, Lewis had a deep-seated loathing for this particular weed and every time he came across it, easily identified by its long, thin, green leaves, he would carefully dig around it, lift the root ball and remove it to the nearest bricked area, where he would carefully place the bulb like a miniature onion on the hard surface and crush it to a pulp with the back of a trowel or a brick.

The soil was another matter. Pale grey talcum powder. In most parts of the garden that's what it resembled before a systematic program of soil renewal was undertaken. To enable the plants to survive over summer, a sprinkler system had sensibly been installed in the early 1980s, but it was not a particularly efficient one and had been used indiscriminately. When I moved in I found that it had been programmed to switch on every second evening at 9 p.m. and, on the first occasion it went into action, it drenched the guests at a drinks party. On another occasion one would arrive home in pouring rain to find the sprinklers going hell for leather, a domestic Antipodean *wasserspiel*, a suburban Versailles. Small wonder that the water bills were astronomical.

But it was not for reasons of economy that the program of soil enrichment was undertaken. To simply bend down and take a handful of soil and run it through one's fingers was to realise that not only had most of the nutrients capable of sustaining plant growth been leached out of the soil, so had most of its colour. It had reverted to something like the original sand that must have covered all of this seaside area except the lush, protected valley. Given its proximity to the sea, one assumes that the soil here would be naturally sandy, but to recognise that fact is not to accept it. Even the sandiest soil can be brought up to speed by regular mulching, but this is something it had not had for years.

The gardener employed for one day a week by the previous lessee had never used waste material for mulch or compost. He simply tossed it in the garbage. Determined that every cutting and pruning from the garden would be recycled, I decided to use a good machine to do the job. Ultimately I would establish proper compost bins, but at this point in the garden's rehabilitation I needed to find an efficient method of converting garden waste into mulch.

I began casting about for a sturdy domestic mulcher – not a piddling little one that choked on any piece of wood thicker than a pencil, but a proper semi-industrial model. I had bought the lease on Bronte House while I was still living in Melbourne and it was there that I found the perfect tool for the job. A keen southern gardener had recommended to me something called the 'Red Roo' mulcher. I liked its

ABOVE: Nothing looks more depressing than a garden at this stage of its life, but there is no substitute for starting from scratch. One has to keep imagining how it will all look once things start to grow.

very Aussie name and was delighted to see that it was indeed Australian made, in a factory in the unlovely Melbourne suburb of South Oakleigh. The manufacturer was an American, one Jim Kerr III from Jackson, Mississippi, a nice chap with a Southern drawl that his decade in Australia hadn't managed to eradicate.

Back home in the States, Jim's family had manufactured lawn-mowers under the brand 'Yazoo', the name of a vanished tribe of American Indians. A few years ago he had had the bright idea of manufacturing garden mulchers. 'After all, sir,' he told me, 'a mulcher ain't much more'n a vertical lawn-mower.' Jim started turning out his vertical lawn-mowers in a modest machine shop, demonstrating their efficiency at expos, garden shows and country field days, where one of his strongest selling points was environmental responsibility.

'We bin' findin' more interest in our products because people are thinkin' more 'bout th' environment,' Jim told me when I was considering the $4000 purchase, and this idea appealed to me. So did the saving. I thought about the time I had rented a mulcher for the day from a plant hire firm and the wretched thing conked out after ten minutes of fitful activity. That exercise cost me forty dollars and delivered a pitiful pile of chips. I calculated that if I bought a Red Roo and it performed each time as well as it seemed to do when Jim demonstrated it to me, I'd amortise my investment after 100 sessions.

Barely a week goes by without this trusty appliance being wheeled out of the shed to chew and shred garden waste into recyclable material, and its first output went into the neo-Bosnian section, later known by the less violent name of the Carriageway Borders (see page 110).

For three whole months the soil was enriched. Beds were turned over and cow manure, peat, vermiculite and slow-release fertilisers dug in deeply. We began digging kitchen waste directly into the ground. A largish stainless-steel container was, and still is, positioned near the sink. Into it daily go eggshells, banana skins, potato peelings, tea leaves, stiffening leftover pasta, chicken bones. Selecting a different position each day and working progressively along the length and breadth of the beds, we were amazed by the speed with which the worms converted everything from carrot tops to crusts into rich, dark soil. As the soil improved, so did the size of the worms, which now approximate the size of small snakes.

But still more work was needed before a single seed could be sown. To check the soil for disease and for missing trace elements, we called in experts from a soil laboratory. In their report they recommended a variety of measures, from boosting pH levels in some parts, to increased use of animal fertilisers to keep soil-borne root diseases at bay.

It's difficult to over-emphasise the importance of this initial preparation or the effect it has had on the present condition of the garden. It involves much work and considerable cost, but the results are there for all to see. And to feel. In these borders you can stoop, grab a handful of soil and it's as fine and as friable as the coffee grounds which, since the installation of an espresso machine, have joined the list of materials dug in.

Later, in 1998, we established a large three-bin compost heap to provide supplementary nutrition. This is tucked away in the remotest corner of the garden to the south-east. Most instructions for composting seem to involve an amount of work equivalent to that required to build a 10-metre fibreglass-hulled cruiser in the backyard. Garden manuals tell us that ideally one needs a base of concrete slabs and four walls, creating three bins, one in which to place the new grass clippings and kitchen refuse, another for the half-rotted stuff and a third for the fully broken down compost ready to spread on the garden. Assuming these instructions applied to European or American compost which, without heat, breaks down more slowly, we skipped the concrete slab, constructing instead three simple wooden dividing 'fences' made of treated slats and attached to large poles sunk directly into the earth. Thus we have a rudimentary version of classic compost bins, one for each stage of decomposition. It works splendidly.

Grass clippings are what are mostly used here – our own and those delivered by a couple of local lawn-mowing services. To these are added hay, straw and small leaves. Cut flowers, when they have wilted and the water in the vases has turned murky, are

OPPOSITE: Each season hundreds of plants are raised from seed and cuttings in an improvised 'nursery' behind the garage.

the garden at Bronte

chopped up by hand with a pair of secateurs and added to the heap, and when large-scale pruning or lopping takes place, the Red Roo is moved down to this part of the garden and the mulched material added to the piles in the bins.

But when we feel the soil needs something really special, we use the caviar of top dressings, a product called 'Charlie's Compost' (see Resources, page 178). It's the finest pre-prepared compost I've encountered: rich, dark, chocolate brown and, yes, even fragrant. Charlie and Rose Hamand, who make the stuff, have it routinely tested by the Sydney Environmental Soil Laboratory to ensure it is of even standard. Unlike some commercially marketed composts that, because of poor ingredients and dodgy quality control, have proved either useless or just plain dangerous, this compost is guaranteed to contain no harmful pathogens and to be completely free from phytophthora, fusarium, rhizoctonia, pythium and other unwelcome diseases. The soil analysis people also report that it increases the activity of beneficial fungi and contains some disease-suppressing bacteria. A little of this magic substance strewn around the base of any plant that looks as though it needs a treat, or a layer sprinkled on top of beds in late winter, after the soil has been forked over and the perennials cut down, and the results are nothing short of miraculous.

There are still a few sandy pockets in the garden, and in these, tough succulents have been planted. But if the garden looks any good these days, it is primarily due to the time taken at the outset to improve the condition of the soil in which so many varied plants now thrive happily.

It would be reassuring to think that one only has to attend to this problem once, but the hard reality is that soil as sandy and as well drained as I have needs constant attention. If proof were needed of this requirement, then one only has to look at the response of the plants to a seasonal top dressing, be it choice compost, mulch or just plain lawn clippings. As steroids are to athletes, so compost and mulch are to gardens.

OPPOSITE: The wooden garage resembling an old barn was built in 1982. However, it looks older, especially when viewed through established trees, vines and perennials. Tithonias and salvias give some feeling for the orange and purple scheme of the Carriageway Borders.

ABOVE: My first task at Bronte was to create light-filled garden beds and dramatically improve the condition of the soil.

beginning the planting

It has been severely subdivided, but the most important section, including natural rock outcrops beneath the house, survives. The east side gives onto grassed terraces apparently reformed with steps, circular concrete pond or flower beds and stone retaining wall. Beneath the wall down the steeply rocky slope is the elaborate rockery garden which, although neglected, is intact with irregular walls and random steps cut or constructed from the rock along the slope. Overgrown plant material: doryanthus, Moreton Bay fig, auracarias, etc.

Condition and Integrity: Overgrown and partly destroyed but enough remains of its unique design to make it one of the most important colonial gardens in Australia.

Description of Bronte House from the Register of the National Estate, Australian Heritage Commission

Rehabilitating an historic garden described as one of the most important in the country is no small responsibility, and the question of what to plant is a contentious one. Historically correct species had been chosen for the 1982 renovation but few had survived. What grows well in one historic garden may do poorly in another. Vaucluse House, the garden of which provided much inspiration, is only a few kilometres from Bronte House and yet plants that

THESE PAGES: It's something of an accepted wisdom among gardeners that seed gathered from plants grown in situ provides better results in terms of vigour and size than seed purchased in packets.

ABOVE LEFT: Myles Baldwin plants out annuals raised from seed.

ABOVE RIGHT: Brendan Lewis, Myles's predecessor as gardener, pots up hippeastrum bulbs after division.

OPPOSITE: Poppy seeds germinate in pots prior to being planted out.

flourish there and have done so for decades keeled over when tried here. The fact that species are known to have been grown successfully elsewhere in the colony in the 1840s carries no guarantee that they were grown here, only that someone else grew them.

I had to make a decision about whether to use what might be called 'period plants' or to use plants that would give a period effect. And I was conscious that here, more than in any other major colonial building, house and garden were virtually inseparable. Gardens were designed to show off a house. Here the garden was planted contemporaneously and always seen as integral to the effect both made on a visitor. Then there was the further consideration that under three separate significant ownerships, the garden had been consistently altered. And some features in the house, such as a billiard and smoking room, simply vanished. Besides, were one to have contemplated a strict period garden around Bronte House, one would have needed to decide which period. Would it be a Lowe garden, a Holdsworth garden or a garden from the time the house was occupied by several generations of the Ebsworth family? If the last, which particular Ebsworth look would one choose, given that they were there longer than anyone else, from 1892 until 1942? There was only limited evidence to lead one towards the plants used during any of these three intendancies.

In the event, I opted for a more relaxed approach: not strictly historicist but then not anti-historicist either. I combined plants that were in favour in the first half of the nineteenth century, plants such as cannas that were much used in the late-nineteenth and early-twentieth centuries, modern hybrids and cultivars of fashionable nineteenth-century annuals such as dahlias (a mania in the 1830s and 1840s), the odd rarity that might have appealed to a horticulturally minded owner, as well as unashamedly modern material.

There is no doubt that the honey bush (*Melianthus major*) was a big favourite with the Victorians, so in it went, along with plain purple iris (*I. germanica*), perky pink and white watsonias (*W. meriana*) and Chinese wisteria (*W. sinensis*). These and other choices would no doubt have the imprimatur of garden historians, as would the single dahlias including the Mexican *D. coccinea*, but I am not so sure about a brash modern cousin, a collarette dahlia streaked white and psychedelic cyclamen. Somehow I feel it would have appealed to those with a taste for the gardenesque, however.

This planting program, though it may sound like fun, was often anything but. No gardener has ever enjoyed one hundred per cent success with everything he or she has dreamed of having in a garden or actually planted. Carefully collected seeds often refuse to germinate, seedlings conscientiously planted in what are, according to catalogues and instruction manuals, ideal positions and with optimum conditions, keel over for no apparent reason. Gardening is about trial and error, but it is also about unanticipated triumphs, which more than compensate for the disappointments.

OPPOSITE: Seed from plants we want to grow again next season are placed in brown paper bags, clearly labelled, tied up with string, hung from coat hooks on the western verandah and allowed to dry before being removed from their pods and placed in small manila envelopes. Not all seed gathered is re-used. Some is produced in such abundant quantities that it is given away to keen gardeners who admire the plant from which it was derived.

For the first year all manner of plants were trialled in the borders. Mrs Lowe had admired the roses in Alexander Macleay's garden, so I planted a dozen or so, including *Rosa* 'Souvenir de la Malmaison', first introduced in 1843, 'Gloire de Dijon', of 1853, and 'Reine des Violettes', of 1860. They looked so pretty in those ubiquitous books on roses, where they are caught by the camera in melting close-up, but flowering was brief and fitful and their contribution to the overall mood and effect of the garden was negligible. They proved to be a sad disappointment. Plants have minds of their own and, like people, often refuse to conform to expected or preordained patterns of behaviour. Many that we thought would love it here didn't, and the mortality rate was alarming.

Those old roses have been replaced by worthier specimens such as *R.* 'Crépuscule' and 'Lady Hillingdon'. Not quite so old (introduced in 1904 and 1917 respectively) as the roses they replaced, they are infinitely better looking and more useful components of the overall ensemble. I also planted numerous 'new old-fashioned' roses, ruthlessly removing the non-performers. Those that now have a permanent berth include a couple of delicious David Austin roses (from The Perfumed Garden, see Resources, page 178), yellow 'Graham Thomas' and 'Abraham Darby', both of which are impervious to salt air but not to attacks from possums.

Climatic conditions were the biggest killers, especially among grey- and silver-foliaged plants. These would look glorious through spring and early summer but, in early January and February, when Sydney's humidity began to kick in, they simply imploded, rotting overnight into tussocks of brown mush. Other plants succumbed to sea spray. Numerous plants have been moved two or three times simply to get them away from the line of fire of the salt air, most notably three mature specimens of *Michelia doltsopa*, which have finally found a spot they like, tucked away in the gully where it is a degree or two cooler than at the upper levels. If all else fails, unhappy plants are simply given away to friends who live miles from the ocean.

The year or two of experimental planting really paid off. The plants that survived this period have kept on keeping on, growing ever more vigorous. The failures have been consigned to a mental file labelled 'Fads, Fashions and Failures'. The garden certainly looked pretty patchy during the period but I now know what will work where. Not that the planting as it stands is immutable. There are, as in any garden, always spots where something new may be inserted by way of a trial run.

So much for theories. I don't have many and remain open-minded about most suggestions. My mission has been to make a garden that suits the house and seems an inevitable part of it. I wanted a garden that seemed to belong to this lovely little building, one with a spiritual as well as a visual connection. Like a long and happily married couple, neither should seem complete without the other.

ABOVE: Strawberries are grown in pots as much for decorative effect as for consumption.

OPPOSITE: A view across the Carriageway Borders to the bay window of the dining room.

OVERLEAF: This is pretty much how Bronte House would have looked when completed in 1845. The colour is original, as is the design for the decorative 'Gothick' woodwork. However, the roof, now slated, would originally have had wooden shingles. During the time of the Lowes's occupancy, the long, low wing to the right of the photograph housed storerooms, bedrooms for servants and the original kitchen. When the road was cut through to the beach, a crude two-storey addition was built to face the street. The circular turret was also heightened with several courses of bricks. The proportion of neither of these additions is happy.

'too hot and too blue'

Too dry, too wet, too sunny . . . For every decision to plant

something in a particular position, there is a cause for

complaint. There are things I wanted to plant that didn't

want to be here, and others that, against the odds, stayed put.

I've found it is best to ignore all criticism, seek no advice,

just do it. And if it doesn't work, do it again. And again. Until

it looks and feels right.

structural plants

Many decisions needed to be made about the planting of the main borders for Bronte House, but the key one concerned structural plants – those plants around which all others could be deployed to best effect. It's rather like flower arranging. One has to start somewhere, and the best way to start is by placing one or two sizeable branches or clumps of leaves in a vase and judiciously placing other material around them. What I wanted was a small number of plants that could be repeated throughout the border and stay put for years, plants with form and presence that would prevent the garden from looking too twee.

The most useful of all the anchor plants introduced in the initial stages of planting, and still performing superbly, are giant clumps of New Zealand flax (*Phormium tenax* Purpureum Group), with leaves the colour of uncooked beetroot. There are six stands of this dotted throughout the borders that surround the circular carriageway, and their inclusion, at the suggestion of Melbourne gardener, writer and designer Michael McCoy, has proved a masterstroke. Their strong, upright form, like clusters of exclamation points, provides maximum contrast with all manner of green plants and 'steadies' the border so that the eye has points of rest while scanning it. In spring, old-fashioned sweet peas (*Lathyrus odoratus*), a seed or two of which were planted at the base of the flax on 17 March (is there any truth in the instruction that these should be planted on St Patrick's Day? Will they perform less well if planted a day earlier or a week later?), are allowed to meander through each clump like Art Nouveau doodles. Later in the year, equally sinuous miniature convolvulus weave themselves through the flax and create a similar effect.

I have made use, too, of the smaller red/bronze/purple flaxes, most notably *P. tenax* 'Anna Red' and *P. tenax* 'Dancer', to which it is first cousin. These smaller flaxes are useful for tucking in the front of the border, echoing both the colour and the form of their taller, grander progenitor.

But bronze- and reddish-toned flaxes are not the only ones used for emphasis. In other parts of the garden, other varieties have been planted. In the borders where the colour scheme is confined to white and yellow, I've used the dashing *P. cookianum* 'Yellow Wave' to provide just that: an undulating wave of strongly variegated yellow and green leaves. I've used it elsewhere, too, grown hard up against rocks and bordering stone steps, and it seems made for each spot. The variegation is interesting. When these plants are young the yellow stripe down the middle of the leaves is most pronounced and the green merely occurs at the margins, but as the plant ages the green colour becomes more assertive. For this reason we dig them up annually, usually in late autumn, remove the older parts and replant the sharp, fresh, yellow ones.

PAGE 72: *Cosmos sulphureus*.

PAGE 73: A sunflower (*Helianthus annuus*).

ABOVE: *Acanthus mollis* is a magnet for snails, but before they move in, the effect of the dark glossy leaves and flowers like oysters arranged on a spike is particularly striking.

OPPOSITE: There is photographic evidence that the verandah on the north-eastern corner of the house was once a conservatory (see page 38). Its use today as a shaded and protected spot for raising a collection of begonias hints at its former incarnation.

When in flower, a near-black stem appears, from which pop scented spider-like pink flowers, with a purple–red back to the petals. So enamoured have I become of this lovely thing that I have it not only in the borders but also in pots – no fewer than six of them, a quartet of them flanking the original entrance of the house and a pair in handsome campana-shaped antique iron urns on either side of the later entrance – so that as one walks around the carriageway, one encounters this plant in various stages of development. A leitmotiv.

But there are other crinums, too – clumps of Cape lily (*C.* × *powellii*) and the local swamp crinum (*C. pedunculatum*), native to the east coast of Australia. This is another glorious plant to which attaches an interesting story.

While directing the Melbourne Festival I agreed to premiere a new work by Aboriginal artists from Broome. I made a trip to the west to attend rehearsals, which were held in the local Country Women's Association hall. It was swelteringly hot inside that fibro building, and at one stage I wandered outside to take some air. On this short perambulation I noticed a superb clump of crinums growing in a public park. One was in flower and the flower was spectacular – huge and as glamorous as an orchid. I nipped off one from the cluster and took it back with me to the hall, where I put it on the piano. Perhaps it was the heat but that single flower seemed to pump out perfume, filling the hall with exotic fragrance. Later I returned to pick over the plant and look for seed but there was none – either on the plants or lying about on the ground. It was a massive clump and, had I brought the required tools with me, I would have dug up a piece surreptitiously from around the base.

ABOVE LEFT: The golden hop (*Humulus lupus* 'Aureus') scrambles up an iron frame copied from a French rose stand. At various times it supports white wisteria, white sweet peas and then the hop is allowed to go on a rampage before being cut to the ground.

ABOVE RIGHT: The glorious flower of the bronze-leafed Queen Emma lily (*Crinum augustum*).

Being obsessive about things like this, I set my mind to getting this particular crinum. I asked friends and relatives heading for holidays in Broome to visit the plant and check it for seeds. They were not able to find any, but several confirmed my memory of this being a remarkable plant and the flowers spectacular.

In the end I did the only thing an obsessive could do. I contacted Lee Cooper, head gardener of Broome Shire Council, and asked her if I could fly over and bring back some bits. And so it came to pass that, in February 1999, I travelled to Broome for a few days, met up with Lee, who picked me up from my hotel in her ute and drove me to Bedford Park, where, in indescribable heat, we dug up half a dozen plants from around the edges of this ancient clump.

Many people admire this crinum. They like the lime-green leaves and are as captivated as I was by the flowers, but more than one visitor has thought it a little peculiar that someone would make a transcontinental flight to the remote north-west of the country just to bring back a plant. In the same way, people can't understand why I like Wagner.

Also incomprehensible to some is my indifference to box (*Buxus*) hedging, which has been one of the biggest gardening fads of the last decade. I did have a number of box plants left over from a roof garden I had in Melbourne and, as I am always loath to throw out a healthy plant, I decided to place small spheres at key points around the carriageway circle. If the clumps of flax act as the exclamation points in the grammar of this garden, then the balled buxus constitute the full stops. There are eight of them, each placed at a point where a path meets the circular drive. They are kept tightly balled and, after each clipping, they put out fresh, juicy lime leaves.

Where the circular drive meets the paths of the garden, the beds come to a point and the small triangular patch between these green spheres and the brickwork edging has been filled with society garlic (*Tulbaghia violacea* 'Silver Lace'). From one small pot of this have come many plants. Its variegated leaves are attractive but even more so are its flowers, lightly but sweetly scented lavender stars held proud of the foliage.

Having visited the recreated Monet garden at Giverny, outside Paris, I was taken with the idea of nasturtiums (*Tropaeolum*) scrambling out of their beds and rampaging across paths. I tried that effect at Bronte, but alas, fungus made a meal of every variety I tried, including the highly desirable *T. majus* 'Empress of India'. Only later did I settle on hardier cultivars that have since thrived.

Then I hit upon a wanton verbena, *V.* 'Homestead Purple', that does what the nasturtiums were meant to do. The story goes that this cultivar survived a century of neglect on a farm in the United States, flowered on in extremes of climate and grew ever more vigorous. This must be true, for here it has demonstrated not only its affability but also its adaptability, sending down roots into the most unwelcoming compacted clay. I keep lifting sections and planting them in spots that can do with a little colour. For six months of the year, this remarkable plant puts out the prettiest of purple flowers – not bloodless mauve or wishy-washy blue, but a clear, bright Tyrian. Were I to move to a smaller garden, there are many plants I would give up, albeit reluctantly, but not this one.

Another leitmotiv perennial, more of a tree really, is the *Brugmansia*, formerly known as *Datura*. This plant, too, has operatic connections.

Several heroines have met horticulturally related ends. In Cilea's verismo, *Adriana Lecouvreur*, the eponymous heroine expires after smelling a bouquet of poisoned violets sent to her by a rival in love. More specifically, in the last act of Delibes's 1876 *opera comique*, *Lakmé*, an exotic tale of a Brahmin priestess in love with an English officer, the houri, whose name serves as the title, commits suicide by chewing on the leaf of a datura plant. The datura (the name derives from the Hindu word *dhatura*) was commonly used in India to stupefy or poison a victim, and flowers or leaves, crushed, then boiled in water like spinach, produce a liquid that, when imbibed, can produce a powerful hallucinogenic effect.

Reclassified now as *Brugmansia*, and popularly known as angels' trumpets, this plant is a spectacular sight when in full flower. Five varieties occur around the Carriageway Borders at Bronte: single specimens of *B. sanguinea* and *B. aurea*, as well as a smattering of *B.* 'Frosty Pink' and the small, white-flowered *B. meteloides* and two fine standardised specimens of the apricot-flowered *B.* 'Charles Grimaldi'.

This last cultivar is a knockout. When I took over the house it was already here – a lank, formless mess, woody beyond words and flowering fitfully. Boldly I cut it to the ground and, as if by some magical subterranean force, a single shoot came rising out, straight as an arrow. A light went on in my head. Why not grow this as a standard? Every other ambitious shoot arising from the mass of roots was mercilessly eliminated, allowing the single trunk to grow tall and thick and strong. Equally mercilessly, all side shoots were removed from the trunk until it reached the desired height, when it was allowed to branch out to form a canopy, the apricot-coloured blooms resembling upturned candelabra or a Balinese umbrella, the flowers exuding a glorious perfume, especially at night – although it is intoxicating rather than hallucinogenic.

Visiting the garden when this was in full flamboyant flower, Colin Smith made a suggestion. Why not plant one at the other end of the façade, for balance? No sooner said than done. A sapling stripped from the mother plant went in the next day and was given the same treatment – fed well but deprived of any opportunity to branch, kept straight and upright till it resembled its parent. The secret, if it may be called that, to having these plants look good and flower spectacularly is to keep them well shaped and hard-pruned. The minute they become leggy, they assume a bedraggled air and the flowers are fewer.

This is probably one of the simplest plants to propagate. Cuttings strike easily and quickly in sand, or a large cutting can be kept in water till it puts out roots. This

the garden at Bronte

latter method has the advantage of looking good while getting going. I put a large glass vase on the windowsill of the kitchen so it catches afternoon sun and watch the stick, at the other end of which I usually leave a few leaves, slowly put forth white tapewormy tendrils that can virtually fill the vase. (In the interest of aesthetics, it's also advisable to change the water regularly.)

These, then, are the larger, constant elements of the garden: a melange of trees, shrubs and grasses, but always repeated, sometimes with variations, just as Wagner did with his leitmotivs.

Filling in the spaces between repeated elements becomes relatively easy, like adding ornament to architecture, and can be done with annuals. Again, two themes recur, two plants keep coming back.

Delicacy and toughness are not always characteristics that go hand in hand but I have found two plants that fit this bill. One is a perky orange cosmos, *C. sulphureus*, which grows everywhere throughout the garden. When the white and yellow borders seem in need of a little jolt, I scatter seeds of *C. bipinatus* 'Purity' into the gaps, and in no time they fill with a filigree of fine green foliage and subsequently produce large, nodding, white daisy-like flowers that glow even at night during summer.

From Thompson and Morgan, the great English seed firm whose seductive catalogue is a recurrent temptation to serious plant persons (see Resources, page 178), I have a superb new cosmos of semi-dwarf habit. It's called *C. bipinatus* 'Daydream' and the flowers are a seductive pale pink with a darker centre. Although its flowers are smaller than most, they are more freely produced over a longer period.

I also grow another charming one, *C. bipinatus* 'Candy Stripe', the original seed of which came from Colorado in the United States. Although the flowers are basically white, they have a picotee edge blushed with bright rose pink and vary slightly with each flower. It's as though someone had taken a felt pen in this colour and loosely outlined each one. The flower is not as big and showy as some, but the plant is tall, which enables it to be placed behind denser foliage and have only the carnival-coloured flowers peeping out from behind. This is fine by me, for, to tell the truth, the foliage of most cosmos is not especially desirable, ergo not worth having to the fore.

The second recurrent annual in the garden is the poppy. I had been told that the previous lessee had scattered poppy seed about for years and, sure enough, during my first spring here, up came rivers of them. Alas, they were pink – the *wrong* pink, the colour of a pink gin – and this particular shade sat uneasily with the stronger, more confident colours now peppering the borders. If the colour was not right, the idea of a slew of poppies enlivening the early spring scene was, so I set about trialling more accommodating varieties, settling in the end on two: a single poppy called *P.* 'Thunder Cloud' and a fantastic double-ruffled one so dark as to appear black.

OPPOSITE: A corner of the Carriageway Borders, where they meet the north-western corner of the house, at its summer best. The show-stopping canopy of *Brugmansia* 'Charles Grimaldi' offers not only visual splendour but also intoxicating perfume at night. Severe pruning keeps the canopy compact and the flowerings profuse.

ABOVE TOP: A single purple poppy, *Papaver* 'Thunder Cloud', surrounded by sweet peas (*Lathyrus odoratus* 'Painted Lady').

ABOVE BOTTOM: White coneflower (*Echinacea purpurea* 'Alba').

'Thunder Cloud' looks the way it sounds: a mysterious, soft purple, the colour of wet slate or of the sky when a storm is imminent, and with a deep bruised purple cross in the centre. The flowers don't last long and a stiff breeze is sufficient to blow off petals that are as thin as cigarette papers, but I wouldn't be without this beauty for quids.

The other is a different matter altogether – a variety not unrelated to the gin-pink ones planted by my predecessor (which still keep coming up), but a garnet black in colour. It's *P. paeoniflorium*, so called for its voluptuous, ruffled peony-like flowers.

Although they don't count as leitmotivs, for they are not planted consistently, I have also used the common Mexican sunflower (*Tithonia rotundifolia*). As poppies and sweet peas and myosotis, the old-fashioned blue forget-me-not that is the most reliable ground-covering annual I can think of, fade and die off, up come these large-leafed plants to fill in the gaps perfectly.

Recently I've begun introducing succulents into the main borders in the interest of strong structure and dramatic contrast with more conventional border plants, and they will be more widely used in future. While their rightful home is in a designated Succulent Garden (see page 136), they have begun to creep westward.

I freely admit that the decision to abandon horticultural apartheid and mix things up a little more was directly inspired by a visit to Wigandia, the extraordinary garden created at Mount Noorat in the western district of Victoria by the ingenious and opinionated William Martin. Martin has opted for an all-bets-off approach to garden design and plant choice and has created a triumphant and highly individual, possibly unique, garden. Caring little for what might be thought polite, and in complete revolt against the hegemony of English gardeners, he merrily mixes all manner of plants in an assured and whimsical manner, and the result is a triumph as well as an inspiration.

This is not to say that Martin has little regard for form or colour. He has a deep concern for the overall effect of every nook of his garden and, while the choice and juxtaposition of plants may be surprising, it is always harmonious. He is not in thrall to a particular colour scheme, but what colour there is, in a garden dominated by glaucous foliage and the red scoria from which it emerges, is subtle and understated, accenting rather than overwhelming the broad forms of the plants he has selected and placed with such daring. There is room in any garden for a surprise or two, maybe even for a joke.

OPPOSITE: Plants common and uncommon from the garden at Bronte.

TOP LEFT: The Mexican sunflower (*Tithonia rotundifolia*) is tough and easy to grow and provides fiery colour accents in late summer through to autumn.

TOP RIGHT: Flowering tobacco (*Nicotiana sylvestris*), distinguished by its noble bearing and sweet scent.

BOTTOM LEFT: The glorious rose-flushed flowers of *Brugmansia rosea* don't dangle like their other brugmansia cousins, but rather kick out in a flighty fashion, rather like a can-can dancer's skirt.

BOTTOM RIGHT: *Salvia* 'Purple Majesty' looks and performs better than lavender.

the hair of the earth

Another recurrent theme in the garden at Bronte House is the use of grasses. Just as clumps of dark flax are positioned at intervals in the borders around the drive, so too are clumps of grasses. Over the past two decades, ornamental grasses have enjoyed increasing popularity worldwide, and for good reason. Few plants are so giving, providing first clumps of fresh green leaves, then feathery heads and, as the leaves die, subtle beige accents among neighbouring green plants. Thus, one has interest for months on end and it is only in the fallow months of July and August, when the dead leaves are shorn off at ground level, that clumps of grasses temporarily cease making their generous contribution to the romantic appearance of the garden.

In a sense, grasses are every bit as valuable in a garden as trees. The great German gardener Karl Foerster poetically and accurately described grass as the 'hair of the earth' and so it is, the antithesis of baldness, growing long and supple, blowing free in the breeze, catching and reflecting different lights.

Internationally, the two most favoured grasses have proved to be *Miscanthus* and *Pennisetum*, but the list does not and should not end there. No garden of any size should be without *Calamagrostis acutifolia*. Its verticality is a major asset, as are its flowers, emerging a smudged, hazy mauve in early summer and ageing almost imperceptibly to a soft cream.

And the show-stopping golden oats (*Stipa gigantea*), which I first spotted in the gardens at Glyndebourne, where a clump was planted to considerable effect at each of the four corners of a cruciform path, is another grass I would not want to be without. A real gob-smacking example is to be seen in Jeremy Francis's glorious borders at his Cloudehill nursery in the Dandenongs, just out of Melbourne (see Resources, page 178). When not in flower, this particular grass is a fairly dreary thing, a low-growing tussock of nondescript leaves like emaciated green vermicelli, but in summer it bursts forth, producing huge wands a couple of hundred centimetres long, from the ends of which dangle buff-coloured oat-like flowers. A mature specimen of golden oats is something to be prized, but one has to be patient. It was two years before the one at Bronte produced its first show, and it will be several more years before it can match the spectacle provided by the Cloudehill or Glyndebourne specimens. This grass needs to be left undisturbed. It looks as though it can be lifted and easily divided but to do so is to risk almost certain loss. David Glenn of Lambley Nursery (see Resources, page 178) at Ascot, near Ballarat, in Victoria, from whom small plants are available, advises thinning dead leaves by donning a gardening glove and gently 'combing' the hair of the grass to remove dead strands. Anything more aggressive can prove fatal.

OPPOSITE: Eulalia (*Miscanthus sinensis* 'Variegatus') is one of the loveliest grasses one can grow. It forms graceful clumps and its feathery flowers resemble the tightly curled ostrich plumes worn by aristocratic ladies when presented at court.

ABOVE: The wing leaves and fat catkins of fountain grass (*Pennisetum setaceum*).

Another stipa worth considering is *S. tenuissima*. This is more reticent than other forms of the grass and, to my way of thinking, most resembles hair – fine and soft and seductive in movement.

Easier to grow, and only marginally less spectacular, are members of the *Miscanthus* genus. In the yellow and white border at Bronte House I installed one called *M. sinensis* 'Silberfeder'. Those with even rudimentary German will know this means 'silver feather' and, true to description, it produces silvery feathers that seem to float above the dark-green leaves of the grass, like plumes on an outrageous Edwardian hat. An added attraction of this lovely grass is the fine rib of silver that runs down the middle of each leaf.

We have planted *M. sinensis* 'Variegatus' which, like many grasses, assumes a more monumental, architectural form with age, and *M. sinensis* 'Sarabande', which has silvery mauve flowers that appear in summer and hang on through autumn and winter with lovely changes of colour. And *M. sinensis* 'Zebrinus' makes an appearance, its long, arching, dark-green leaves banded with yellow, giving it the look of those

exotic striped timbers such as Brazilian rosewood, coromandel, satinwood and albura used to such dramatic effect as inlays or cross-banding to enliven the brown mahogany in Georgian furniture.

Mondo grass (*Ophiopogon japonicus*) has made the sandstone blocks used as steps at either end of the lower rainforest area look as though they have been there forever, which they haven't – only since 1995. And we planted some of the even more modish black mondo (*O. planiscapus*), but have not yet found the right position for it. I can't get excited about this novelty grass. It looks too much like squid ink pasta to me, but I do like Japanese blood grass (*Imperata cylindrica* 'Rubra'), which the influential American landscape designer James van Sweden has used to such telling effect. Whereas one good plant of a stipa, a preferred miscanthus or a tufted grass can look good alone, with this one you need heaps. Van Sweden uses great swathes of it in foreground planting and the dramatic red leaves give any garden real punch.

Much of this tale of the creation of the garden at Bronte involves hunting down rare plants, not simply because this is the instinctive method of operation of all collectors, whatever their passion, but because the true collector always likes to avoid the pedestrian, to discover (or rediscover) the neglected or the overlooked, things that have about them a point of difference. In seeking out the exotic and unusual, the gardener sometimes has a particular effect in mind, but he or she can, on occasion, exhibit a wilful kind of horticultural one-upmanship.

I confess to a similar sin as well as to obsessive pursuit. In the first months of the new millennium, I finally got hold of the grass I had most wanted to grow. While in Atlanta for the 1996 Olympic Games, I saw a particularly lovely ornamental grass with beautiful bronze foliage. It was used extensively in public planting there, and a clump of it formed the tail in a curious and none-too-attractive horticultural sculpture in the form of a cockerel in the otherwise tasteful Atlanta Botanic Gardens. Americans are not big on correct botanical names and simply referred to this beauty as 'red fountain grass', although it is certainly not the red of the Japanese blood grass but rather a purple bronze with the distinctive cat tails of most pennisetums. I eventually established that it was *Pennisetum setaceum* 'Rubrum' and hunted it down on the Internet, hoping I might legitimately import seed or plant but was able to do neither.

Apparently it does not grow from seed but is propagated by division, which means a mother plant is needed. It is something of a nightmare trying to import living plants, especially grasses. Quarantine officials fear they will spread the way many others have done, the most notable being the invasive kudzu, or Japanese arrowroot (*Pueraria montana*). Imported to America, it is now known as 'the plant that ate the South' and is virtually ineradicable. I became resigned to living without my purple fountain grass, when suddenly something described as *Pennisetum setaceum* 'Burgundy Giant' turned up in the first catalogue of 2001 from Digger's Seeds in Victoria. It is not quite the same thing, not quite as fine as the true 'Rubrum' I'd first seen in Atlanta and which looks so tempting on a number of online plant catalogues. According to Clive Blazey of Digger's (see Resources, pages 178), importation is too costly and time-consuming to warrant the effort, a fact confirmed by David Glenn, who had in fact imported *P. setaceum* 'Rubrum' only to have it sit in quarantine for months untended. Under such circumstances it is not surprising that it died long before receiving the bureaucratic imprimatur.

Another recent introduction to the garden is kangaroo grass, which I grow in the giant version known as *Themeda gigantea*. It is not a grass for either the faint-hearted or for the foreground. However, with its gigantic stalks, it makes a spectacular impression if planted at the back of a bed.

So flax and grasses form the spine of the garden, the key elements of the borders. Both look good for most of the year, and the fiddling, the additions and subtractions, the trials and the errors, can go on around them without the borders ever looking too naked.

Your average Eurogarden has months of looking dire, with brown earth from which no sliver of green protrudes, and bare trees. There is neither need nor excuse for any such bleak period in an Australian garden. With a little planning, one can have a look of one sort or other for at least ten out of twelve months, and one of the methods of achieving a sense of fullness is by selective use of ornamental grasses.

ABOVE: Two views of the beautiful Japanese blood grass (*Imperata cylindrica* 'Rubra'): top, cut to the ground ready for lifting and separating, and below, with the striking foliage that gives it its name.

OPPOSITE: A rush of grasses in the White and Yellow Borders. You don't need a vast array of flowers to make an impact. Here, yellow rudbeckia, yellow coreopsis and white ginger do the trick.

the garden at Bronte

colouring in

Some friends of mine once stayed in a resort at Port Douglas. As they checked out and signed the visitors' book, they scanned, as one does, the pages for observations from long-departed guests. One in particular caught their eye: an entry from a couple from a village in Wiltshire with an inexpressibly twee name. In true condescending British upper-crust style, they had written in the space reserved for comments five words: 'Too hot and too blue.'

I have often thought of this odd remark while working in the garden. Yes, our climate is hot and dry, which makes it difficult, at least in most parts of this continent, to grow the sorts of plants beloved of English gardeners. And it is blue, our sky often unusually so, a particular blue that, of all our artists, only Arthur Streeton was able to capture perfectly on canvas. It's bluer than one gets in Greece or Italy, an unabashed, unequivocal true blue.

What 'hot and blue' means for the gardener is that we should know our climate and conditions and not, in our horticultural pursuits, slavishly ape English or European manners. I happen to think that the coffee-table garden book, with its ethereal hazy snaps and reproductions of picture-perfect borders that, if the owners are lucky, last a month, has been the primary curse upon Australian gardening.

Now I freely confess, at least in the early days of creating a garden at Bronte House, to an attempt to achieve the wishy-washy Anglo effect. As I have mentioned, in the first months I planted things like *Rosa* 'Souvenir de la Malmaison', so pretty in those rose books where it is seen in melting close-up, but when it flowered, as it did very nicely, I was appalled by its anaemic appearance. In the hard Aussie light it looked wan and ill, with the pallor of a consumptive. Against a cerulean blue sky ('too blue'), it made no impression whatsoever; a chalky blob and the fierce sun ('too hot') quickly compounded the problem of its dreary appearance by scorching the outside petals to a soft umber.

Rapidly I came to the view, advanced by Christopher Lloyd, that greatest of gardeners and honourably exempted from general strictures about English garden writers and their books, that bold colour and form are what one should be looking for, not cottagey effects. Or, if one really has to have the latter, then mimsiness should be mitigated by positioning soft, hazy plants against dramatic, sometimes over-scaled foliage. Fluff on fluff is a no-no. Fluff against solidity and form has real appeal. Thus *Gaura lindheimeri*, attractive enough in its way and passable when planted against lavender, takes on an infinitely more interesting character when set alongside, as I have it in the side garden at Bronte, the massive, greyish sabre leaves of *Dietes robinsoniana* or stiff, fat,

ABOVE: Leaves of spade, spear and spike shapes make for a lively display of foliage.

OPPOSITE: Why settle for one when you can have two? Colin Smith's idea to plant a second brugmansia gives the façade double impact.

lime-green clumps of swamp crinum and underplanted with native plectranthus (*P. argentatus*), a plant much used here and one of the few greys that will do.

Anglo gardeners seem terrified of any bright, clear colour. Unused to too much sun, they don't understand properly how bright, clear, uncompromising colours work in the bright, clear, uncompromising Aussie light. I remember reading the scribblings of some precious English gardening guru complaining about a pansy called 'Jolly Joker'. Quite popular here these days, part purple and part orange, but for this bloke who had first spotted it at the Chelsea Flower Show, it was at one remove from hell. He thought the colour combination so ferociously vulgar that 'one would need welding goggles to look at it for any length of time'.

Quite by chance, purple and orange was the colour scheme for the last Melbourne Festival I directed in 1996, and we asked the Melbourne City Council gardeners – the best in the country – to devise an appropriate and conforming scheme for the beds outside the Victorian Arts Centre on St Kilda Road. They planted the beds with purple violas on one side and orange on the other, with a wide band of *Viola* × *wittrockiana* 'Jolly Joker' down the middle so one colour appeared improbably to drift into the other. The effect was spectacular, and Melbourne, during the period of the Festival, turned on warm, sunny weather, 'too hot and too blue' for those English visitors to far north Queensland, but perfect for a city in the midst of a season of celebration. And no-one seemed to be wandering around wearing welding goggles.

A few English gardeners – not many – share Lloyd's view of colour. The poet James Fenton, who has a garden in Oxfordshire, says the English garden experts have it in for orange and claims that ghastly good taste is 'keeping gardeners away from colours and flowers that give great pleasure, the reds and oranges that, as Constable said, "fire a gun" – things like nasturtiums and Californian poppies and the Mexican sunflower'.

I should make it clear that I am not a colour theorist. Many gardening books supply formulae for polite, harmonious combinations of tints, often complete with charts and colour wheels so you can avoid horticultural solecisms. This may work for some people but not for me. I believe the best effects are often achieved by accident or by trial and error rather than by plan. That is not to say one shouldn't establish guidelines. Popping in every plant you like in every colour you fancy is a recipe for disaster, but rules should not be hard and fast. If it looks good to you, then go with it. If a plant jars or is not a good neighbour, junk it.

Nevertheless, it's reasonable to have some kind of colour scheme to work to, not rigidly, and the one I lit on for the Carriageway Borders has worked pretty well. While not designed to be prescriptive, it was a help in focusing on a particular palette and eliminating nonconformist specimens from consideration. That colour scheme was a Diaghilevian one: purple and orange like the municipal planting scheme in Melbourne,

OPPOSITE TOP LEFT: The plant commonly known as wandering Jew (*Tradescantia fluminensis*) is a weed, but in this beautiful beetroot and grey–green form, it offers generous and showy contrast at ground level.

OPPOSITE TOP RIGHT: Cannas, too, work well when the bronze leaves of a showy tall form are up against those of a medium-sized green one.

OPPOSITE BOTTOM LEFT: The glorious orange flowers of *Spathodea campanulata*, called the African tulip tree for obvious reasons.

OPPOSITE BOTTOM RIGHT: Like some majestic spider, flowers of *Crinum augustum* emerge pale pink from beetroot-coloured buds.

ABOVE: The pale mauve spherical flowers of the globe thistle (*Echinops bannaticus* 'Taplow Blue') are somewhere between a dandelion and a thistle.

but with all of the sub-shades (light and dark mauve, slate, blue–purple, purple-ish red, bronze–beetroot, and tangerine, brick, apricot, coral, pink without blue and the odd spike of alien colour) included. Mr Fenton would like it.

At one end of the orange spectrum there are the cannas, the glorious orange–scarlet flowers of the African tulip tree (*Spathodea campanulata*), which seems to bloom for months in late summer, and the fiery orange of the Mexican sunflower, lighting up the borders at summer's end. But this electric shade of orange is used sparingly, with good, gutsy apricots the prevailing colours in the two roses, *R.* 'Abraham Darby' and *R.* 'Crépuscule', the former planted in multiples along a fence to tangle and writhe through a clipped wall of Chinese star jasmine (*Trachelospermum jasminoides*), and the latter scrambling over an arbour where it vies for attention with a snail vine of approved mauve (*Vigna caracalla*) and a pink-tinged dark-apricot honeysuckle.

The fabulous giant honeysuckle (*Lonicera hildebrandiana*) has proved a triumphant choice to mask an uneasy moment in the house's architecture. When the two-storeyed façade to Bronte Road was constructed, the surviving south-west tower was crudely heightened with rows of brick which looked incongruous sitting atop the original curved sandstone blocks. To mask the join I planted this wonderful giant Burmese version of the humble honeysuckle. A single stem runs up a wire to the point where stone meets brick and then moves horizontally to hide the join. Branches have also been trained on wires stretched horizontally along the crude façade of the late-nineteenth-century addition to the house, and they do much to mitigate its brutishness. The apricot flowers are giant versions of your regular honeysuckle and are equally fragrant, almost as heady as those of the brugmansias scattered throughout the border, the most colour-conforming of which is *B. sanguinea*, with its flowers more like fat cigars than the usual angels' trumpets and orange–red shading into a warm apricot, both colours evocative of the tones of convict sandstone bricks.

In fact, sometimes this garden appears to be all orange – molten and full of fiery flowers. That is mainly in late summer. Earlier, in spring and at the beginning of summer, it is positively purple-ish, with lilac-coloured pentas, Easter daisies, poppies and echiums, buddleias and salvias, rudbeckias and echinops, smashing wisterias and an old forest bell bush (*Mackaya bella*), all in full floriferous flight. Even when the beds are at their most orange, the eye can be drawn to something mauve, especially when the rare and beautiful *Worsleya procera* is in flower (see page 114).

But there are colours other than oranges and purples and apricots and mauves in the garden, for this is not a rigid colour scheme. I cannot live without *Beaumontia grandiflora*, and even though the flowers are non-conforming white, as are those of the star jasmine, gardenia, magnolia and murraya, it has its place scrambling over the garage, its magnificent leaves alone sufficient reason to grow it. The gardenias are orphans.

ABOVE TOP: The simple but striking daisy-like flower of the Mexican sunflower (*Tithonia rotundifolia*).

ABOVE BOTTOM: One of the many forms of liliums grown in pots and positioned around the garden to enliven a dead spot or moved indoors to scent a room.

OPPOSITE: The old-fashioned sweet pea *Lathyrus odoratus* 'Painted Lady' is a sport of the early 'Matucana', the purple and blue colouring replaced by pink and white. Here it meanders through a near-black peony-like double poppy (*Papaver paeoniflorum*), part of an early spring display.

Rather than chuck them I used them to cover a low brick footing for the garage. Sarah Guest once told me she always planted a gardenia bush by the front gate and that's where mine are, all six or eight of them, formed into a hedge so guests arriving get a nice whiff of something other than Dynamic Lifter. The cultivar is *G. augusta* 'Florida'.

And I must admit to the odd pink in the form of the pink-tinged modern rose, *R.* 'Pierre de Ronsard', which has a decidedly old-fashioned look, and *Brugmansia* 'Frosty Pink', the flowers of which are tinged with lolly pink and resemble the ruffled petticoats of can-can dancers. Neither of these pinks is entirely to my taste, but the plants are and they have been allowed to stay, whereas others that worked less successfully with the overall scheme of things have been cruelly excised, unceremoniously uprooted and given to someone less picky than I am.

Does this concern for inclusion of only 'approved' colours sound obsessive? Probably. There is a tale of a Sydney designer whose apartment was all white. A dinner guest brought him some white roses, but instead of admiring them and putting them in a vase as ordinary folk might, the designer looked at them aghast and cried, 'But they're the wrong white!' In a way I can sympathise. Sometimes I look at a bed and think it's as close to perfect as I can get it, except for that dahlia that has come up red instead of orange. Painters must sometimes feel the same way as they wipe off a dab of clanging colour. For a gardener it's simpler. Cut off the flowers or remove the plant.

ABOVE LEFT: The homely echinacea (*E. purpurea*). When the petals drop one still has interest in the remaining rust-coloured spheres.

ABOVE RIGHT: A lovely unnamed single white poppy that just happened to pop up among a swathe of purple ones.

OPPOSITE TOP LEFT: As pretty as any iris or orchid, the lively flower of *Canna* 'Wyoming'.

OPPOSITE TOP RIGHT: The subtle and beautiful claret and white collarette *Dahlia* 'Dandy'.

OPPOSITE BOTTOM LEFT: An unnamed day lily in cherry with a yellow throat.

OPPOSITE BOTTOM RIGHT: A single dahlia (*D.* 'Yellow Hammer') whose golden petals are streaked with amber.

a period plant

A visit to Vaucluse House in Sydney is always an inspiration (see Resources, page 178). Bit by bit, bed by bed, the garden's nineteenth-century aspect has been recreated, down to a new kitchen garden in which grow only varieties of known pre-1850s vegetables.

Even without knowledge of garden history one can sense a different feel about this garden. Where else can one see an arch of woven dried tree branches like a thick inverted scribble of the letter 'U' spanning a path and with the lovely old-fashioned snail vine meandering through it?

But of all the nooks and crannies at the Vaucluse House garden, the thing that for me most evokes the Victorian era is a wire plant stand filled with potted begonias. This is placed just to the left of the public entrance to the house and, if one were to photograph it and print the picture in sepia, it could pass for an early image of a display of plants that our ancestors thought of as indispensable. Everything about it seems perfectly in period – the stand, the handmade pots, the position in shade but with both light and heat, and the plants, which are now horticultural period pieces.

Once fearfully fashionable, begonias are rarely seen these days in private gardens and hardly ever in nurseries. Nor are there any recent publications on them so, although I grow two, maybe three, dozen varieties (there are over 900 in all, according to the Begonia Society of New South Wales), I know the names of only a few. As was the custom a century and a half ago, they were collected as cuttings or in some cases just single leaves and grown on from there.

I, too, have arranged begonias in the Vaucluse House manner, on two antique tiered French stands made of steel and wire. These have the advantage over the more usual English wire ones of having zinc troughs that fit inside each wire section so that the run-off of water doesn't rust away the wire.

When I was about ten, my Aunt Nell showed me how to propagate begonias from leaves. She would lie a leaf on a pot full of sand, burying a little of the stem in the sand and pinning the leaf down flat using long glass-headed pins. Then she would take an old blue Gillette razor blade and neatly cut the ribs of the leaf, explaining that this procedure helped the new growth establish at the point where they radiated outwards from the stem.

I follow this method but find neither the pins nor the razor blade make much difference. The leaf can simply be held in place by the sand. Most begonias are a breeze to strike, either by the leaf method or from more substantial pieces of stalk, and that is how I got cracking on my collection.

The finest specimens now at Bronte House came from Bob Cherry, who collected them in the wild from all over South-East Asia. Bob couldn't supply names for the

OPPOSITE: Recesses behind the stands where I keep my begonias may originally have been windows, since blocked up, and there is evidence of a door in the far wall. It is possible that the entire northern side of the house, to the left of the formal entrance, was, at one time, a kind of open loggia.

ABOVE: The house always seems welcoming.

specimens he procured and neither can I, although I am happy to oblige visitors to the house with a cutting or two. These begonias come in all shapes and sizes. I have one with a large, round, lime-green leaf speckled with yellow that looks fantastic among the other more regularly encountered specimens whose leaves tend to be British Racing Green, that lovely dark colour that in a certain light can pass for black. In that category I have specimens with enormous tall canes that brush the wooden lining of the verandah on which they grow, and others of more modest habit that compensate for size by producing trusses of gorgeous flowers in a range from white to fire engine red. The flowers are a bonus. I would be happy to grow begonias just for the foliage, for the occasional spotting and marking, for the infinite variety of leaf shapes, for their ineffably Victorian look, but they have other singular advantages.

Once established and if correctly positioned to avoid exposure to direct sunlight, they are relatively fuss-free. Regular watering and occasional fertilising with Maxicrop (a natural seaweed-based all-purpose fertiliser that a number of gardeners I admire swear by, as do I) is all they get from me, and once a year they are reorganised. Those that have grown too tall are planted out in a shady section of the garden where, given a free root run, as well as rich moist soil and a minimum of direct sunlight, they are even more vigorous, some growing up to 2 metres.

With their annual clean-up comes fresh soil, thinning of the ones that seem crowded in their pots and a general reordering of position. The ones that grow tall are placed on the top shelf and interspersed with lower-growing varieties with contrasting leaves. In the middle row of the stand are placed pots of the aforementioned lime-leafed variety because of its habit of growing downwards so the wonderful mottled foliage is displayed in full-frontal fashion. On the lower shelves are the more delicate specimens, some with fragile pinkish stems and wan small leaves among which lurk reticent small pink flowers. It's a knockout display, some fifty pots in all, producing not just a fine show but additional plant material for other nooks and crannies in the garden.

As the begonias thrive, the larger ones, moved into the shaded lower sections of the garden, tower above the visitor. Mention the word 'begonia' to most gardeners and they picture either flashy, tuberous varieties that were the staple of the Victorian conservatory, or drab, nondescript forms. Never for a moment do they imagine just how varied, subtle and, yes, spectacular these plants can look if treated lovingly and without too much reverence.

I am sure that some of the varieties I have are not 'historically correct' in that they are relatively recent discoveries. At Vaucluse House they have been very strict about what is allowed to grow. In my historic garden I am more flexible and more than one modern hybrid has found its way into the beds, but the begonia, in all its astonishing forms, seems somehow to belong to and evoke a different era.

ABOVE: The flowers of the beautiful begonia.

OPPOSITE: This area on the eastern verandah is used for outdoor lunches and dinners, but, given that it contains a large table, it also serves for sorting and packaging seeds and for potting and staking. Note the mis-matched sandstone blocks, evidence of an opening in the end, indicating the possibility of a transverse walk. This would allow residents to take exercise in inclement weather.

OVERLEAF: The view to the sea through the arches that define the White and Yellow Borders.

a walk through the garden

This house has lots of visitors – not only the hundreds, and sometimes thousands, who come on open days, but the smaller groups from garden societies as well as international visitors. I have evolved a particular kind of traffic flow, bringing guests on a by-now well-trodden path that allows for both a comprehensive inspection and a goodly number of surprises. So in describing each section, you can perhaps form an idea of how all the bits of house and garden fit together.

the carriageway borders

The first view most visitors have of Bronte House and its garden is from the entrance gate by the garage to the left, and the first impression is of the series of beds of varying size that ring the circular entrance drive: the 'Carriageway Borders'.

By far the most dominant element in this panorama is the circular lawn, roughly 18 metres in diameter and slightly mounded. Because of its size and monochromatic nature, extreme measures were needed if it was not to overwhelm all around it, hence the inclusion of powerful sculptural plants in the beds surrounding it. Now the eye moves easily and naturally across the lawn to the densely packed beds.

To integrate the garage, with its simple timber structure and barn-like appearance, better with the garden, its brick foundations have been masked with two rectangular hedges of *Murraya exotica*, grown and clipped to precisely the point where the boarding begins so that the wooden structure seems to float on a green base. The simple wooden steps to the garage door are flanked by a pair of standard wisterias (*W. floribunda* 'Kuchibeni'). This is the only serious touch of formality in these borders. From here on in, around the entire circumference, informality and mass are the hallmarks.

The width of the beds varies wildly, from less than 1 metre to around 3 metres wide, and yet there is an illusion of both depth and uniformity. We had to play many tricks to create this illusion. Giant specimens were planted close to the edge, and extremely tall plants such as tree dahlias beyond the back wall of the border, just where the land slopes steeply down to the gully. Many traditional European borders are straight with brick walls as background. We had no such luxury and no architectural enclosure, so any sense of the beds curving in orderly fashion around the drive is illusory.

PAGE 108: Common purple lantana invades the iron slats and curves of a Regency bench.

As the beds curve around, they embrace buddleias, cannas, grasses and flaxes, plants of every sort and size, from ground-huggers to towering 3- and 4-metre-high background plants. The contrast in leaf form is amazing, from the large, folded grey leaves of the honey bush (*Melianthus major*) with its dramatic pinked edges, to the simple, narrow spears of Louisiana iris (*I.* 'Dural White Butterfly').

PAGE 109: Day lilies (*Hemerocallis*) and Queen Anne's lace (*Anthriscus sylvestris*) in the White and Yellow Borders.

ABOVE: Myles Baldwin trims the circle of alternanthera around the lemon tree on the small patch of lawn to the west of the house.

Over the first arbour through which the visitor passes as they enter from the west grows a melange of apricot roses and a soft apricot and pink honeysuckle of unknown variety. It was culled from an old garden and is part of the general conspiracy to hide the arbours under a tangle of plants. The second arbour is similarly treated with roses, lemon-scented jasmine (*Jasminum azoricum*) and small purple convolvulus. This archway leads to the White and Yellow Borders, but if one bypasses it and moves on around the Carriageway Borders, one encounters clumps of orange cannas, Russian sage (*Perovskia atriplicifolia* 'Longin'), *Iris pallida* 'Variegata', purple cranesbills and

OPPOSITE: Thin but looking thick. The bed in which these plants grow is at its widest no more than 1 metre, narrowing to a few centimetres. However, layered planting and the positioning of large specimens well forward in the beds create the illusion of considerable depth.

amethyst-coloured alstroemeria. A certain symmetry prevails here. At either end of the façade of the house are the previously mentioned apricot brugmansias. Flanking the front door are symmetrical clusters of pots stuffed with crinums, phormiums and ornamental oxalis. The narrowest bed is just past the front door, a tiny strip of earth carrying an admirable weight of planting.

On the verandahs on either side of the front door are the great rarities of this garden: the significant specimens of *Worsleya procera*. Of all the plants in the garden at Bronte, the worsleya is the most special. My friend Judy Cuppaidge raised it from seed and coddled it for a decade or more before it came good with a flower. It moved with her from Paddington where it grew in a pot, to Church Point where she planted it in the ground, then to North Sydney where it went back into a pot. It is a temperamental thing, flowering pretty much when it feels like it, but whenever it decided to do its thing, Judy would ring and I would travel, usually at 6 a.m., to see it in all its glowing mauve glory. The flower head emerges on a sturdy, flat stem from the heart of the plant and its marvellous scimitar-like leaves seem to part for its arrival. It happens quite quickly; the calyx opening to reveal five, six, seven, sometimes eight buds that open in quick succession.

After visiting Bronte House for the first time, Judy rang to tell me she was giving me the plant. I could not believe her generosity. Here was a plant she'd lived with for over three decades. She was parting with it to someone she knew and liked but who had none of the personal associations with it she had, for she had not only grown it but

ABOVE LEFT: The glamorous leaves of the indispensable *Canna* 'Tropicana' are as good-looking in a vase as they are in a garden.

ABOVE RIGHT: The honey bush (*Melianthus major*) was grown in colonial gardens, but even if it weren't, one would still want it for its pleated and pinked leaves and unusual soft grey–green foliage.

painted and drawn it many times and showed it off to friends. It was duly transported from North Sydney to Bronte and put in a beautiful pot.

The worsleya rewarded me by seeming to die. The curved leaves went as limp as wet feathers. Judy saw it and confirmed that it was ailing, so one fine Saturday morning, with the help of three other people, it was gingerly lifted from its pot, the roots bathed in Fongarid, the pot washed and sterilised and the worsleya replaced in a new, freer draining mix of scoria, crushed bark and a little sand. It was also given a miracle fertiliser from the United States on which it had been nourished since infancy. The combination of better growing conditions and familiar food did the trick. It has grown to about double the size it was when it arrived here, and in one twelve-month period produced no fewer than four flowerings. This, I discovered later, was because it had decided to bifurcate – transform itself into two plants, each of which flowered twice.

The colour of the worsleya is unique and it seems to glow in the way the flowers of the tree dahlia or the jacaranda do, as if subtly illuminated. Of all the mauves in the garden, the flowers of this rare lily are the mauvest.

The worsleya has had a great number of names. For years this member of the *Amaryllis* genus was classified as *A. procera*. Later its name was changed to *Hippeastrum procera*, and later still it was called *H. procerum* (sic) and was even known as the Blue Hippeastrum, even though its colour is closer to mauve than blue. Recently it has been reclassified as *Worsleya rayneri*, and again as *W. procera*, and is now acknowledged to be a monotypic genus as it has never successfully been crossed with any other member of the *Amaryllis* genus to which it belongs.

Western botanists first stumbled across it in the nineteenth century in Brazil where it grew in the Organ Mountains north of the bay of Rio de Janeiro, often in narrow crevices of earth no more than 30 centimetres wide, its roots deep in the basalt, its leaves continually bathed in mist. The natural habitat of the worsleya is confined to an area about 2 kilometres wide near the summer resort of Petropolis, some 750 metres above sea level. It is now virtually extinct in the wild in Brazil and is a considerable treasure elsewhere. It was collected by French and English botanists, including one Arthington Worsley who cultivated it in England and whose name it now bears. Because of its imperial colour and the splendour of its flowers, it is also known as the Empress of Brazil, but old-time Aussie gardeners, ever eager for a diminutive, used to refer to it as the Blue Hippie.

In this garden it is a show-stopper and gets the VIP treatment it deserves. If there is one wildly anticipated event here, it is the flowering of the worsleya. Hushed groups of visitors are admitted to admire it as one might a newborn baby. Friends are contacted and they come to marvel. In 2001 we managed something that had not been achieved before: a crosspollination between the two mature plants, which had obligingly flowered simultaneously. This resulted in the older specimen setting seed, and to date over 100 seedlings have been raised.

Continuing around the Carriageway Borders, one meets other smaller relatives of the larger worsleyas: baby clumps potted up and placed on either side of the secondary entrance to the house, further evidence of the favoured treatment this plant receives and its preciousness.

Along the western service wing of the house an assortment of aloes and agaves have been planted to disguise an agricultural drain, and very nicely they do, too, in what is virtually pure gravel.

Set in the grass in the adjacent triangle of lawn are three citrus trees: a lemon, a lime and a mandarin. In Georgiana Lowe's time, and later, a substantial kitchen garden was maintained at Bronte House. In the 1982 renovation, James Broadbent indicated this by planting the citruses in neat circular beds. To keep out encroaching lawn grass and maintain perfect circles, we sank flexible strips of dark-green plastic curled into rings into the earth around each tree. By way of decoration, we ringed each circle, the shape mimicking in miniature that of the huge central lawn, with wrought-iron hoops. A Regency conceit this, the idea is to make the flowers that grow within the circle seem to be contained in a large, flat basket. Humphrey Repton created something similar for the gardens of the Royal Pavilion at Brighton. His were intended for mixed annuals. Mine simply define 'doughnuts' of clipped alternanthera.

And so we have come full circle. From one gate to another, around borders that have the look and feel of tradition but are, I feel, both eclectic and idiosyncratic.

OPPOSITE: The most splendid and rare plant in the garden at Bronte, *Worsleya procera*. Everything about it is sensational, from the form and the ribbed leaves to the glorious flowers in a colour best described as fluorescent mauve. Soon after this photograph was taken, the plant bifurcated, turning into two magnificent specimens. It also obligingly set seed for the first time in its fifty-year life.

ABOVE: The exotic *Zinnia* 'Candy Cane', seen here in two forms, is a multi-coloured cultivar developed in the United States in the nineteenth century, which is perhaps why it looks at home in the garden at Bronte.

the eastern terrace

With this curious house it's difficult to decide which is the front and which the back. The front might be the side that faces the sea, but the other side is also the front in that it is where visitors enter, so let's call the seaward side the 'eastern front'. It sounds both bellicose and pretentious, but it's a fair description. And so the considerable rectangular expanse of lawn on two levels in front of the house from which one has glimpses of the Pacific becomes the 'Eastern Terrace'.

Today this is the least intensively cultivated part of the garden, mainly because most of the area is occupied by a large croquet-sized lawn. At some unknown time between the departure of the Lowes and the end of the nineteenth century, probably during the Holdsworth occupancy, one of the owners of Bronte House decided that a velvety-green sward was the appropriate setting for a gentleman's residence and laid the turf. To do so was a considerable feat as the ground fell away steeply from the house and a retaining wall had to be erected about 13 metres from the steps leading from the verandah. This was constructed of massive sandstone blocks, rough hewn on all but the outward-facing sides, which were appropriately rusticated. Because of the sheer weight of soil that needed to be packed behind to make a level lawn above, the wall was heavily buttressed to prevent collapse. All this construction was done in and around existing rock formations, so much of the natural appearance of the surrounding area, if not the natural form, was retained. However, it does seem like a significant intervention and one would almost forego the lawn, lovely though it is, and incredibly useful for entertaining, to have the natural rocks still in place as they are in the area between the wall and the boundary fence and beyond, where Mrs Lowe made what she called her 'Woodland Boudoir'.

Short of tearing up the lawn to create gardenesque beds as proposed by Broadbent, there was not a great deal of gardening to be done in this area. A pair of balled box (*Buxus*) were set either side of the steps from the verandah, seaside daisy (*Erigeron karvinskianus*) stuffed into crevices in the sandstone paving to spill out its perennial froth of white daisies, and the long thin bed running between lawn and wall was also stuffed with agapanthus. However, to the right as one faced the sea, there was a bed that cried out for attention.

Now it so happened that I had a pair of antique Regency wrought-iron garden seats that, when put together, formed a perfect concave semicircle. The bed was of roughly this shape, so I decided to make something more of it than a repository for diseased plumbago and out-of-control lantana. The soil was built up to form a bank that nicely contoured to accommodate the old benches, from which it slopes gently upwards providing a lushly vegetated backdrop. By another stroke of luck, a *Magnolia grandiflora*, planted in 1982, had been perfectly positioned in the centre of the bed so one was able to plan somewhat formal

ABOVE: Hardy, self-seeding and in that happiest of colours, orange, *Cosmos sulphureus* is a winner.

OPPOSITE: In keeping with the nineteenth-century tradition of constructing a fence from twigs and branches gathered on the property, this fence on the Eastern Terrace has been made from bamboo cut and milled on the property. It isn't a permanent structure, nor is it meant to be. As soon as it begins to weaken, it will be replaced with the same material and in an identical design.

OPPOSITE AND OVERLEAF: Early photographs show various kinds of urns used to adorn the eastern lawn. The first was a large single-cup-shaped one set dead centre on the upper part of the lawn, framed by the central arch of the decorative woodwork on the verandah. Later, when the steps were inserted, a pair of campana-shaped classical vases with handles were placed on the plinths at the bottom (see photograph, page 39). Currently, a set of three matching white marble urns have been placed in this area, a pair on the plinths and a third in the distance to mark the entrance to the pathway to the lower parts of the garden.

arrangements of plants on either side: a brace of echiums (*E. candicans*), a couple of bronze-leafed castor-oil plants (*Ricinus communis* 'Altropurpureum'), two clumps of the invaluable native Gymea lily (*Doryanthes excelsa*) and, for ground cover, lantana and rose-scented geranium, plus a few clumps of ornamental grasses, to keep the bed looking full into winter. When spring comes, I let the vinous plants run free and geranium, nasturtium, and lantana romp through the back and slats of the old seat. A thick clump of exquisite miniature gladiolus from Lord Howe Island burst forth at the right-hand side of the seat to charm anyone able to find room to sit amid this tangle of greenery and flowers.

To the right of this bed, a small flight of rustic steps leads down to the lawn. These were flanked by a pair of *Viburnum tinus* that were cut to the ground and, when regrown, trimmed into fat balls. Disappointingly, they fell victim two years later to bracket fungus and have now been replaced with oleanders. Another single oleander with carmine flowers already stood in a circular bed directly against the house. It had grown immense and flowers were sparse. At this size it was impossible to thin so it was pruned to the ground. People are often aghast at this radical form of pruning, but it works a treat, and the old unnamed oleander is now something of a feature.

By the side of the house is a large, old *Camellia japonica* with pedestrian pink flowers that are tolerated rather than loved. It, too, has been tidied up, given a simpler form and now looks far more respectable than it did when I moved in. Nothing grew underneath, so I planted a carpet of native violet, a plant which merges easily with the adjacent lawn and ensures the entire area is greened.

Behind the semicircular seat and matching bed, runs a brick-edged path that is certainly part of the original traffic system in this garden. A tricky task to plan and plant this, but Michael McCoy had an inspired idea. He suggested planting, in random fashion and in a frenetic

assortment of colours, clumps of every canna I could lay my hands on. We agreed that the effect could be horrendous but decided to give it a go, risking total colour chaos even further by combining the majestic cannas with two kinds of salvia, *S.* 'Black Knight' and *S.* 'Indigo Spires'. Far from being a flop, the bed is a triumph: show-stopping but not for the faint-hearted.

Two of the best cannas were swaps. One exceptionally tall variety, dubbed *C. brasiliensis* by Brian Morley, Director of the Adelaide Botanic Gardens whence it came in exchange for some rarity or other here, towers well over 3 metres. The flowers are piffling orange things and are not why I grow it. It's the height that counts, and the lush pale-green foliage. The other beauty is *C. iridiflora*. Unlike its cousins, whose flowers are big and blowsy, this one has beautiful cyclamen-coloured trumpets that dangle in clusters from pendulous stems. Better still, it is a 'period' plant, and may well have been grown here at some time during the nineteenth century.

Cannas not winkled from friends or coaxed out of council gardeners came from a specialist nursery in Ringwood North, Victoria, called Canna Brae Country Garden Nursery (see Resources, page 178), run by an enthusiast named Anne Glancy. Her list is a winner, with each canna described faithfully by colour and form and the catalogue neatly divided into heights. It's not one of those glossy nursery catalogues filled with glamorous but slightly unreal colour photographs and hyperbolic descriptions, but rather a simple photocopied list with good, clear descriptions, which probably explains how Anne can offer her plants at such a low price.

BOTTOM LEFT: Four or five varieties of fuchsia grow in large square tubs along the eastern verandah.

BOTTOM RIGHT: *Erigeron karvinskianus* is better known as the seaside daisy because of its affable habit of flourishing in coastal conditions. Here it grows in crevices in the steps leading down to the Eastern Terrace.

OPPOSITE TOP: There are times when this lovely Regency semicircular seat almost disappears under a tsunami of nasturtiums, rose-scented geranium and lantana.

OPPOSITE CENTRE: A view of the house from the fountain area.

OPPOSITE BOTTOM: An early-nineteenth-century cast-iron Val d'Osne bench features a picturesque Gothic design popular at the time.

Over the three years that this Canna Walk has been in existence, only two problems have occurred. The first is the rust that tends to disfigure the leaves at the end of summer, developing perhaps because of persistent humidity and lack of air circulating through this densely crowded space; however, half the impact is that very congestion. As one walks along this path, giant plants loom overhead, flowers in salmon, orange, scarlet, some speckled, some streaked, are right there, literally in your face, while the salvias below spill out in a riot of blue. And so the rust is endured for the sake of the vigour and theatricality this planting affords for almost four months of the year. The second problem is – or was – yellow. Two or three of the clumps of cannas were yellow-flowered varieties, and although we were after a jangle of colours, the yellows were just a tad too riotous. Open a pack of Smarties, tip the contents out onto a table and remove the yellow ones and you'll see what I mean. A riot of colour is fine but the yellow seemed to tip the effect from vulgarity towards anarchy and so the offending plants were relocated.

A few other plants were introduced on the Eastern Terrace: some red and orange alstromeria; a lovely China rose called *R. chinensis* 'One Thousand Lights' from nurseryman and botanist Bob Cherry; and a few chirpy dahlias, including a brash collarette variety (*D.* 'Festival') in white splashed with puce that is a particular favourite, mainly because it makes the bed in which it grows look less polite.

If the main borders around the drive, on the southern side of the house, are planted with orange and purple flowers, and the walk connecting this area to the Eastern Terrace almost exclusively in white and yellow, the beds to the east are a deliberate mishmash of hotter colours. Given the expanse of green lawn and tree tops as far as the eye can see, some contrast was needed. Not quite the famous red borders at Hidcote Manor Garden in Gloucestershire, but pretty good nonetheless.

Behind the agapanthus planted at the edge of the lawn is a charming rustic bamboo fence made from canes of the giant bamboo that were cut, milled and sawn on site. Before that, the agapanthus alone served to delineate the space as well as send signals to the incautious not to proceed beyond this point lest they plummet over the edge. And to add a little more clash and clangour to the colour scheme, throughout the agapanthus are planted drifts of *Cosmos sulphureus*, grown from seed obtained in the Netherlands and now self-sown in profusion right along this perimeter bed. Come November, the combined effect of the agapanthus and cosmos in flower is striking. The aggies tower over the cosmos that pepper the potentially dull run of strappy green leaves with bright orange flowers and go on looking wonderful long after – almost two months after – the last bright-blue mophead of flowers on the agapanthus has withered and the dried stems been cut down.

A bonus is that the cosmos produces seed in abundance. All of my friends have been given some, and on open days when people ask (as they inevitably do) what is that marvellous orange flower, they are presented with a small packet of seeds which I have rather cheekily christened *Cosmos sulphureus* 'Bronte House'.

ABOVE LEFT: The colourful collarette *Dahlia* 'Festival' verges on the vulgar. Its white petals appear to be painted with bold stokes of cyclamen.

ABOVE RIGHT: Another colourful collarette, the Mexican dahlia (*D. coccinea*).

OPPOSITE: Hippeastrums potted up ready to move into the house. These beautiful bulbs are kept in a cool room and potted progressively so as to have an almost continuous supply of flowers for the house.

the white and yellow borders

It's a bit rich describing these two beds as borders. In England, a border is something roughly 100 metres long. What I call the White and Yellow Borders flank a straight path, not much more than 17 metres from end to end, with relatively narrow beds on either side. It is a transitional area and as such seemed to need a slightly calmer treatment than the larger spaces at either end.

When I first took over the lease on Bronte House at the end of 1994, the form of the garden existed, that is paths had been laid and the formal areas given an immutable shape, but there were no demarcation points in the garden, no features that signposted the progress from one section to another. The only piece of garden architecture to be seen was the skeleton of a garden arch. Rusted and warped beyond repair and held together by a combination of the tangled tendrils of long-dead vines, it spanned the pathway at the north-western corner of the garden leading from the Carriageway Borders to the Eastern Terrace. However, early photographs show rustic fences and other forms of timber supports for plants, all long vanished.

Almost the first thing I did was to commission four new arches, exactly the same height and width as the surviving one, though of simpler construction, since the manufacture of fancy wirework garden ornaments and arches is now an almost lost art. (I have heard of a woman in the Sydney suburb of Rozelle who does make some smaller pieces.) Constructed of steel and with sturdy wire mesh between the uprights to support climbing plants, the new arches are very plain with no falderals or fancy bits. However, to chime with the style of the house, they were formed not as the conventional inverted U-shapes but with a subtle Gothic form akin to the design of the supports on the front and back verandahs. In shape they are not dissimilar to arches surviving at Kippilaw, an historic house and garden just outside Goulburn in southern New South Wales.

Deriving from *arbor*, the Latin word for tree, an arbour can signify simply a shady, grassy spot within a garden or an orchard, but nowadays it is most commonly used to refer to any construction of wood or wire on which plants or vines can be supported. The great advantage of any such construction is that it can mediate between the lower-growing shrubs and annuals used in most gardens and taller shrubs and trees in the background. Few garden beds or borders contain plants higher than a couple of metres, while trees in the background can shoot up to six or seven, and few plants are available to fill the sometimes gaping space in between. I've found the solution is to use some form of support to take plants high above ground level and thus provide not only contrast but the variation needed for really interesting borders. Michael McCoy often emphasised

OPPOSITE AND OVERLEAF: Two views of the White and Yellow Borders. Old-fashioned shasta daisies (*Leucanthemum × superbum* 'Aglaia' and 'Snow Lady') are allowed to ramble over the path and day lilies (*Hemerocallis*) in several different colours of yellow from butter to pale pumpkin float over the lower plantings.

ABOVE: Before and after – the seed pods of Madagascar jasmine (*Marsdenia floribunda*) are filled not only with seed but also with fine, silk-like floss, and the flowers emerge beautiful and waxen.

to me the need for height, achieved both naturally and artificially, and his advice has not gone unheeded.

One of the four new arches was positioned where the old collapsing Edwardian model had stood, spanning the path that leads to the garden shed and beckoning the visitor through and beyond. Another two were positioned at the northern side of the house and serve a dual purpose. They frame, beautifully, the view of the sea beyond and define and enclose the White and Yellow Borders. The fourth, a somewhat narrower one, straddles a path that leads to the composting and work areas at the south-eastern corner of the property and neatly disguises what could be a fairly unattractive part of the garden. But the two on a straight north–south axis at either end of the White and Yellow Borders are by far the most conspicuous, ergo the most important. To the eye, one virtually sits inside the other and they create an illusion of greater depth to this area than is the case (see back-cover image).

Never one to do things by halves, I've planted not one but three or four plants to trail over these frames. As mentioned previously, on one arch, the beautiful honey-scented yellow David Austin rose, *R.* 'Graham Thomas', romps up and over from both sides, totally indifferent to the salt-laden winds that blow directly from the ocean beyond. Intertwined among its branches are a *Marsdenia floribunda*, another marvel from Madagascar (often called Madagascar jasmine) whose clustered flowers are ravishingly scented and whose big mango-like seedpods dangle attractively in the space below, as well as lemon-scented jasmine. Imagine the combination of these three fragrances on a balmy summer night when the heat of the day has stirred their secret perfume production facilities!

Over another arch grows *R.* 'Lady Hillingdon', shot through with more jasmine, and to these are added in spring a riot of sweet peas, and later a charming small morning glory (*Convolvulus* 'Milky Way'), which is pure white but with a purple star and throat. It is through this

arch that one enters the White and Yellow Borders, and there are plants at this point that have features in common with the garden we leave and the one we enter. A large *Hibiscus glaber* grows at this point; a transitional plant, its bronze leaves relating to the round borders and its yellow flowers hinting at the colour scheme beyond.

To achieve height in the wider bed of the White and Yellow Borders, I placed two tall French wrought-iron rose stands equidistant from each end. Now there are quite tall plants in this bed, including white and cream gingers, yellow cannas and the 2-metre-tall *Rudbeckia californica* 'California', but the stands, some 3 metres tall, tower above them. Resembling outsized Victorian pot stands, and traditionally used to display climbing roses, they now support white wisterias that grow up inside the tapered frames and tumble out over the tops. No sooner has the wisteria finished flowering and been cut back hard (usually in January), than the stands are covered with the beautiful golden hop, *Humulus lupus* 'Aureus', which rampages up the centre and sends its tendrils out as envoys to spread joy through neighbouring plants. When in full flight, these towers of sharp gold–green leaves look spectacular, points of near-fluorescent colour against the homelier greens of the surrounding plants.

In this bed grow the old favourite honey bush, oyster plant (*Acanthus mollis*), white cleome (*C. hassleriana*), a large-flowered apricot day lily (*Hemerocallis*), and another with flowers the colour of pumpkin, together with one of the loveliest plants of this region, the Lord Howe Island wedding flower (*Dietes robinsoniana*).

In the bed opposite are two plants that were here long before I came and will be here long after I have departed. One is a lovely old frangipani, the common *Plumeria rubra* that flourishes in thousands of suburban gardens throughout Australia, rarely tended and appreciated as it deserves to be. Its opposite number at the other end of the walk is a venerable old *Strelitzia nicolai* that provides heft and mass. This bed runs along the northern side of the house, and one of the reasons for choosing a predominantly white colour scheme and laying such emphasis on fragrant plants is that the bow window of the dining room butts out into the garden bed and I wanted to have plants outside these windows that 'read' at night and were fragrant, for there is nothing more sensuous than dining in summer and being able to both see and smell the garden outside.

Cestrum nocturnum grows underneath the window. It is not a pretty thing and is tucked away out of sight so it can be smelled but not seen. In spring and early summer, a cavalcade of white lilies emerges here too: the regal lily (*Lilium regale*), November lily (*L. longiflorum*) and their more exotic cousin, the snowy-white variations on the golden-rayed lily of Japan (*L.* 'Rubbrovittatum Apollo'), *L.* 'Casablanca', *L.* 'Taj Mahal' and *L.* 'Siberia', all with intoxicating perfume.

Throughout the garden I have made extensive use of wires to train vines in desired directions – not ordinary wire, but stainless-steel wire purchased from a ship's

OPPOSITE: The philosophy of maximum foliage contrast in action, with the leaves of each plant dramatically contrasted with those of its neighbours.

ABOVE TOP: Yellow liliums are planted throughout these borders for seasonal colour, dutifully rising through the mass of foliage in summer for a splash of colour and fragrance and then waiting patiently below the leaf canopy for next year's display.

ABOVE BOTTOM: Another exotic occasional bloomer, the spider lily (*Hymenocallis caribea*). It's worth growing just for its bold blade foliage, so the white flowers are a bonus.

chandlery, stretched between eyelet hooks and with a steel turnbuckle to keep it taut. By fixing a T-wire, one can train a vine to any desired height with the stems kept absolutely free of side shoots entwining the upright wire. When it hits the horizontal wire that forms the top part of the T-support, I let the plant go for its life, providing a splash of airborne greenery and colour. This form of wire support is relatively inexpensive, especially when compared to trellis, and is infinitely more durable. Further, it's just the shot for plants with pendulous flowers.

My showpiece plant handled in this style grows in this bed, a vigorous Indian thunbergia (*Thunbergia mysorensis*) that forms a high boa of greenery from which dangle spectacular racemes of saffron and red cupped flowers. It lives against the wall at the back of the southern bed of the White and Yellow Borders, and its survival has something to do with the fact that it is protected from wind and salt by an adjacent architectural feature, the quaint octagonal tower, the only one of this shape, at the corner of the building. But there may be another reason why it has flourished. On the other side of the wall where it grows is the drawing room whose fireplace is active in colder months, so the wall is kept heated throughout the few cooler months that masquerade as winter in Sydney. In England, in Europe and even in Tasmania, I have seen hollow walls against which fruit trees are espaliered. Behind the wall is some kind of furnace arrangement that pumps warm air into the space between the walls so that the fruit will ripen beautifully and not be carried off by frost. In a totally unplanned way, this is the effect I have at Bronte. I am not so sure that this special showy plant would survive a really cold spell, but it's reassuring to know it will not be put to the test.

There are other places in the garden where vines turn in high-wire acts. Alongside the Indian thunbergia grows an almost identical vine, though with red flowers, *T. coccinea*. Inspired by Georgiana Lowe's watercolour that shows an unidentifiable vine growing through the Gothic woodwork on the front of the house, I've 'wired' these spots and planted below a pair of Fraser Island creepers (*Tecomanthe hillii*). On wires along the paling fence fronting the street flourishes the blue sky flower (*Thunbergia grandiflora*) while inside the weird and wonderful giant Dutchman's pipe (*Aristolochia gigantea*) trails along the fence above the compost bins. Wire allows one to add another dimension to gardening – the airborne horizontal.

ABOVE: A rare form of the old cottage garden favourite, Queen Anne's lace (*Anthriscus sylvestris*). The flowers are pale chartreuse, instead of the usual white that earned this delicate plant its popular name.

OPPOSITE: Autumn crocus (*Zephyranthes candida*) enlivens a section of the White and Yellow Borders with its captivating six-petalled flowers. Entwined through it is the small *Convolvulus* 'Star of Yalta'.

OVERLEAF: A view of the Succulent Garden from the top of the steps leading down to it. The rustic seat is a choice example of colonial bush carpentry and came from the remarkable collection of primitive Australian furniture formed by Lord Alistair McAlpine.

along the hidden path

From the main garden area at street level, three paths lead to smaller garden areas on lower levels to the south and north. The most obvious method of descent is from the Eastern Terrace via the pathway leading to the fountain. If instead of powering ahead you make a left turn here, you drop quickly into a garden that, while on an infinitely more modest scale, reminds me of the French and Italian Riviera.

the succulent garden

Like the gardens of the French and Italian Riviera, the Succulent Garden and Lovers' Walk are set on a steep site and make much use of rocks and succulent plants. The three most notable examples of gardens of this type are La Mortola, also known as the Hanbury garden; Clos du Peyronnet, the Waterfield garden; and Major Lawrence Johnston's Serre de la Madone, all created by English gardeners who clearly itched to grow the exotic plants of other climes. I do not delude myself that my modest spread is in the same league as these ambitious gardens – heaven forbid, for the maintenance on them would bankrupt a Rothschild! – but it is reminiscent of them, not only in the repertoire of plants but by the fact that planting is dictated by the steep seaside site comprising massive rocky outcrops that tumble downhill to the flat area of the public park beyond the boundary gates.

Into one great lump of sandstone were carved, presumably by convicts attached to the Lowes, a series of rough steps to provide access to ground level. On the other side of the boulder is another set of steps, these made of rubble and mortar to facilitate circulation. When the current hectare of land was fenced off from the park, it was done in a rather insensitive fashion. Precious remnants of the garden – a circular planting area, considerable amounts of dry-stone walling and, most valuable of all, Mrs Lowe's Woodland Boudoir to which she frequently alludes in correspondence, all now lie outside the boundary fence. A more sensitive and sensible plan would have been to include these in the curtilage, even though they would have marginally reduced the amount of open space available to the public.

Ample evidence, including photographs and drawings, exists of these rocky areas, but it is difficult to discern what was actually planted in and around them. I have opted for succulents. Poor soil and the absence of an irrigation system were two determinants here. As it turned out, the planting has been hugely successful. As one descends by sloping path or steps, giant furcraeas loom overhead. These were here when I arrived and continue to flourish, although when they reach full maturity they send up huge green lances spangled with flowers that are both stunning and saddening in that the plant dies immediately after flowering. To lose giant plants such as these is a depressing experience as they have such a confident presence and take years to reach maturity, so I always collect and plant all of the tiny flowers that fall round the base, for each is potentially another spectacular giant.

More theatricality is provided in this area by two other superb and under-utilised plants, *Pachypodium lamerei* and the dragon tree (*Dracaena draco*). The first is from that treasure house of unusual plants, Madagascar, and is sometimes known as the Madagascar palm. It has a curious trunk not unlike an elephant's but is covered all over

PAGE 134: A beloved bromeliad: *Vriesea hieroglyphica*.

PAGE 135: The Lovers' Walk.

ABOVE TOP: *Echeveria elegans*. The fetching roseate forms of this genus of succulents make excellent ground cover.

ABOVE BOTTOM: *Echeveria × imbricata*.

OPPOSITE: This is where one begins the descent into the Succulent Garden. All of a sudden, polite and pretty plants give way to dramatic forms and colours.

with aggressive-looking spikes. From the top shoots a mop of thin green leaves, and its flowers, which appear in the centre of the cluster of leaves, look uncannily like those of the ordinary, everyday white and yellow frangipani. I first encountered the Madagascar palm in the Royal Botanic Gardens in Sydney. A friend who spotted it there told me he thought it the ideal specimen plant for a particular spot in the rock garden where it would be seen in the round.

Now I happened to be driving through Paddington one day when I saw a magnificent example growing in a pot on the paved verandah of a terrace house. The Botanic Gardens examples were single-branched specimens; this one had three amazing trunks and its Jurassic shape was perfect. After dropping by several times I eventually found the owner at home and asked him if he wanted to sell it. It had outgrown, indeed cracked, the pot in which it grew and the owner knew he would have to do something about it. To my good fortune he relinquished this rarity for a fraction of the price it might have brought at a swanky garden shop. And, of course, it proved to be just the shot for the spot we had in mind.

What had grown there before was one of my least favourite plants. The list of plants I loathe is relatively short for I feel that, given the right spot and the proper context, any plant can look good, but I do loathe with a passion the Cocos palm (*Syagrus romanzoffianum*). There were two quite large examples of this particular palm growing in the garden at Bronte House when I moved in and I counted the days until I could see them off. However, the gardener at the time, Brendan Lewis, was fanatical about palms – an enthusiasm I share, which may be why I was able to set aside my prejudices and allow

flowers, at times as many as a hundred. This was an import, a specimen of some considerable age acquired from that great authority on orchids, York Meredith, whose fabled greenhouses, now vanished, in the Sydney suburb of Cromer were an Aladdin's cave of treasures. However, it looks, as do others that were similarly located during the nineteenth century in or around rocky outcrops in the gardens of Admiralty House, Kirribilli, as though it has grown here forever.

There are three additional clumps of rock lily at Bronte, one perched in the fork of a venerable old Port Jackson fig (*Ficus rubiginosa*), another two set at ground level. There was a fourth, the second largest of this quartet, and it had been judiciously placed to take the eye from the specimen in the tree to the plant at one's feet, to the superb old specimen on the big rock and beyond to one on a smaller rocky outcrop. Alas, someone spotted it in full flower and found it so irresistible that he or she scaled the fence and nicked it. To prevent further theft of rare or advanced plants I have installed three rows of razor wire above the chain wire fence and have begun to cover this entire metal barrier with anti-personnel plants such as bouganvillea.

The *Dendrobium speciosum* var. *hillii* is not the only orchid grown here. Small pink rock orchids (*D. kingianum*), as well as clumps of the so-called crucifix orchids (*Epidendrum ibaguense*) in red, orange, mauve, purple and yellow and the exotic *Zygopetalum intermedium* also flourish in this space.

Gardening being a matter of trial and error, it is also about conservation. I try not to waste anything and certainly not to discard useful plants. When presented with a cymbidium orchid, I have, when flowering is over, planted it out despite the fact that the foliage is so lethally dull. In this way a couple of trough-like beds made on top of

ABOVE: The path that leads from the Succulent Garden back up to the Canna Walk.

OPPOSITE TOP LEFT: A striking unnamed canna cultivar, speckled red on yellow.

OPPOSITE TOP RIGHT: A pair of moths mate on a dramatic red canna with yellow edges to the petals.

OPPOSITE BOTTOM LEFT: One of the most beautiful of orchids and so easy to grow is the zygopetalum from Brazil. And as if its flamboyant colours were not enough reason to have it, it possesses a delicious fragrance.

OPPOSITE BOTTOM RIGHT: This unnamed succulent begins life as a soft cream with pink edges and gradually darkens to grey–green.

rocks by setting stones on edge and cementing them in place, then filling the enclosed space with soil, were quickly filled, but the conditions were not ideal for the orchids, nor did the foliage look especially interesting. Cymbidiums are best grown in shade houses and tend to perform poorly in the rough.

Zygopetalums are not nearly as fussy as cymbidiums. I was given one of these in a pot in Melbourne and in a few years it grew to fill two much larger pots, so the offspring were pressed into service as replacements for the sulky cymbidiums. Whereas the cymbidiums demand growing material, the zygopetalum is semi-epiphytic and will thrive on fresh air or the next best thing, a light, fibrous, well-drained mix of loam and peat moss or sphagnum. And there can be no doubt that the flowers of this orchid are more exotic, the petals greenish yellow, blotched with a brown–red or purple-ish brown. The doyen of gardeners and garden writers, the late Russell Page, once advised a gardener against mean plantings: 'Don't plant one, plant a hundred,' he said. So now, instead of a tutti-frutti assortment of cymbidiums, there are two bold beds of this beautiful native of Brazil. At least a hundred of them.

There is one other feature of this curious and crowded space I call the Succulent Garden, and that is a rockery dating from the last quarter of the nineteenth century. When I first saw it, it was smothered in bromeliads which were unhappy at having been placed in such a scorching spot and showing their displeasure in a myriad of browned-off leaves. When I cleared them away for relocation, I discovered underneath a perfectly preserved rockery, complete with clusters of coral and rocks honeycombed by the waves and clearly fetched up from the beach. In form, this bed, set in the middle of a path that divides and reconnects on the other side, greatly resembles a similar rock-bordered bed in the garden of Glenholme at Ballarat, Victoria, a house built in 1871. A small amount of resetting of loose stones, and this was ready for planting with a select group of specimen succulents.

The entire Succulent Garden is predominantly dry and well drained, but the porous nature of the sandstone means that there are areas that seem forever moist. Here grows a beautiful *Selaginella kraussiana*, a small-leafed ground-covering fern rather like upmarket moss, that tumbles down steps and is happiest in dark, damp corners that are lit up by its bright acid-green foliage.

That I have been able to grow so many exotic plant specimens in this garden is simply because of the topography. I am grateful for this because the mood in the Succulent Garden is altogether different from the trim and manicured beds above. While nowhere on the same scale, it has a smidgen of the flavour of Le Jardin Exotique at Monte Carlo. That famous garden has a similar repertoire of plants and is arranged in a rocky area overlooking the sea.

And there's another amusing association with the Mediterranean state. In recent years, house prices in Bronte have skyrocketed and the area is now referred to as Bronte Carlo.

OPPOSITE: As well as five types of orchid, day lilies and soft ferns, bolder subjects have been slipped into crevices in the rockwork. These include no fewer than eight different types of frangipani, in colours from peach to blood red.

ABOVE: A most exotic thing indeed, *Pachypodium lamerei* from Madagascar, with its menacing trunk armed with spikes and a mop head of leaves from which emerge clusters of frangipani-like flowers.

the lovers' walk

What a corny name this is. We don't use it much but to do so can be justified by history.

Before the creek that ran through the gully below the garden on the northern side was converted into an ugly concrete stormwater drain, the path alongside it was known as The Lovers' Walk. It is designated thus in the 1882 subdivision brochure and described as 'a romantic and shaded walk parallel with the ravine running towards the sea'. The accompanying sepia photograph chimes with a watercolour painted in 1885 by a minor Australian artist, William Andrews, and inscribed *Lovers' Walk, Bronte*, now hanging in the house. Both show, in effect, a rough track through natural bush with mature trees on both sides. Identifiable in the photograph are ferns and Gymea lilies (*Doryanthes excelsa*), while among the loosely painted trees in the watercolour is a grass tree (*Xanthorrhoea australis*), which may well have been the one Georgiana Lowe recorded forty years earlier (see page 30). From this material, Glenn Stevens of the local volunteer bush regeneration group was able to identify five species indigenous to this particular valley.

But this earlier walk was well below the level of the walk in the current garden, which runs parallel to it and for which we have no name. We usually simply refer to this area nowadays as the rainforest section as there are numerous rainforest species flourishing here and it is dark and cool, especially on a summer's day.

In 1994 it was virtually impossible to traverse this part of the garden. There was no proper path, just a dirt clearing on the side of the slope, along which one scrambled at a forty-five-degree angle like a mountain goat. Nor was there any planting of signifi-cance. When a curtilage was carved out for Bronte House in the early 1980s, a fenceline was established here. As I have said, it might have been wiser to demarcate a larger area of garden and incorporate more historic remnants of Mrs Lowe's layout, but it seems that security was the issue and the powers who made the decision opted for a boundary and fence high above the floor level of the gully.

One of the few rational bits of inherited planting was along this fence. By way of a screen, someone had planted a long line of *Alpinia zerumbet*, a tall-growing plant with curious flowers that resemble a cross between small eggs and orchids. Known as shell ginger, it is much cultivated in Hawaii and valued for its density and durability. Unchecked, it had grown too dense here and has recently been thinned, driven back to a single line along the wire fence, which it conceals perfectly.

One tends to put off difficult tasks, and this part of the garden, being on a perilously steep slope and in the worst condition, was tackled last. The bank was severely eroded. The area seems to have been used as a kind of dumping ground for all kinds of rubbish. Just as the northern side of the gully had shamefully served as a tip for building

ABOVE TOP: Shell ginger (*Alpinia zerumbet*) comes with either plain or variegated leaves and produces clusters of egg-shaped flowers that open to reveal an orchid-like throat.

ABOVE BOTTOM: When the flowers on the vast swathe of clivias on The Lovers' Walk fade and die in late August and September, up come spires of November lilies (*Lilium longiflorum*) that extend the flowering period in this area to almost four months.

OPPOSITE: When the path was laid along The Lovers' Walk, the plant of choice to both clothe the bank and ensure soil retention was the humble clivia.

waste during the construction of one of the hideous developments that has disfigured Bondi Junction and earned it the name Bondi Jungle, so, on a domestic scale, this southern slope had been treated as an outdoor litter bin.

If there had ever been a retaining wall for the beds above, it had long since vanished, so the first task was to install one. Using traditional dry-stone wall techniques, a long, low wall was created behind the upper borders that, in addition to defining the beds, prevented the soil being washed down the slope during storms. Whenever and wherever we dug spades, we struck broken bottles, rusting cans, shards of crockery. Some form of planting to hold the bank was urgently needed and the simplest and most effective was the shade-loving clivia. Had I had access to a vast number of the old-fashioned drooping clivia (*C. nobilis*), with its Christmas bell flowers, I would have used this variety, but it proved impossible to buy in any quantity, so I settled for *C. miniata*, which is less refined but was also much used in old gardens. In all, a staggering 3500 of these were planted on this slope, their fleshy white roots tangling into a mass and preventing erosion. When they are all out in flower, usually in late August or early September, they make a marvellous sight – a carpet of orange and dark green.

To avoid banality in this mass planting, certain small areas were carved out for more unusual varieties of this same plant: a fine unnamed hybrid with tall leaves, probably the result of an accidental crosspollination that had emerged in an earlier garden I made at St Kevin's, a Queen Anne Revival house in Woollahra, and which I have propagated into a respectable clump; clusters of broad-leafed varieties, usually known as Belgian hybrids, which have showier flowers including one lot where the flowers are fiery red; and a drift of the rare and beautiful yellow-throated cream ones. The creaminess and yellowness of these vary considerably, but the group is generally known as *C. miniata* var. *citrina*.

The clivia requires almost total shade. In order to shelter it from the sunlight still able to penetrate the relatively dense overhead branches and leaves, a median canopy of *Cyathea cooperi* was introduced. While perhaps not as fine or as gutsy as that other great Aussie tree fern, *Dicksonia antarctica*, of which there are also several examples in this part of the garden, *C. cooperi* is useful in that it grows rapidly and its great fronds provide wonderful dappled shade as opposed to gloom. Rising nobly from the carpet of clivias at various points in the bank, clusters of these tree ferns create a handsome layered effect in a difficult-to-handle area.

Once basic planting was established, some even more serious work had to be undertaken. There were no steps at either of the two ends by which one accessed the walk; it was just a kind of goat track of tamped earth. It was perilously steep and in wet weather became so slippery that to attempt to either ascend or descend was to invite at best a sprained wrist or ankle, at worst a broken limb.

Old photographs of Bronte House in the State Library, undated but probably

taken in the late-nineteenth century, show a kind of conservatory arrangement built out over the southern verandah on the entrance side of the house. It must have been very functional – the perfect place to raise seedlings and cuttings – but it was pretty hideous and has long since been removed. However, three courses of sandstone blocks, clearly put there to support the glass panes of the conservatory, remained and gave the house a lopsided look that the Lowes would have found as distressing as I did. By removing the stonework and extending the verandah posts it had supported all the way down to ground level, elegance and symmetry were restored to the façade and the area is now used, as it were when smothered in glass, as a place for propagating material for the garden.

The removed stone blocks did not go to waste, for they were recycled as steps to facilitate descent to the lower garden. At both ends, the steps were given interesting angles and curves. At the bottom, a flat path bordered with huge blocks of treated timber was created, with a step or two along its length to prevent it from looking too much like an airport runway. Earth was dug from the slope, the wooden edges put in place and the earth replaced or used to make the path level or to build up the bed below. The visitor now descends into this cool and quiet section of the garden via stone steps, some barely visible in the froth of grass and creepers planted to make the passage look natural, to a pleasant walk some 80 metres from end to end.

Strolling from east to west, one encounters first a small collection of bromeliads. Indeed, the beginning of the walk is signposted by a pair of campana-shaped terracotta urns in which are planted two of the most spectacular bromeliads imaginable, *Vriesea hieroglyphica*. On open days at Bronte House I often stand on the lawn with pad and pencil and issue similar equipment to all helpers, for I know from experience that one will be asked the name of this or that and can then oblige by writing it down. I must have written down the name *Vriesea hieroglyphica* hundreds of times.

One happens across marvellous plants in a variety of ways. Sometimes one sees in a book or catalogue a photograph of a plant that takes one's eye. At other times friends tell you about something they think absolutely perfect for your garden. Unusual plants are encountered (although not so often in these days of aggressive marketing of disposable plants) in nurseries. But most often they are seen in other people's gardens. I know this from experience.

I first saw this variety of bromeliad in the garden made by Duncan McKellar at Fernleigh near Byron Bay. There, too, they were grown in pots flanking a path to a pool with a central fountain, the top basin stuffed with a lush planting of the striking streaked arums, *Zantedeschia aethiopica* 'Green Goddess'. This was an effect I would love to have copied, but instead had to satisfy myself with getting the name of the striking bromeliad and the very next day heading out to a nearby specialist nursery where Duncan had bought his to see if they had any more. Fortunately they did, and it's difficult to imagine any plant that would look better than they do at the entrance to this particular garden path. Formal in shape, they have concave, outward-curving leaves of the sharpest chartreuse green, with irregular horizontal markings that resemble ancient hieroglyphs, hence the evocative description that has been attached to them.

On this same excursion to what must surely be the most amazing bromeliad treasure house, Pine Grove Nursery, in the small town of Wardell (see Resources, page 178), I also picked up some other beautiful specimens: two plants of *Neoregelia* 'Johannes Royal Burgundy', and the exotic *Hohenbergia corriao-arauji*.

When clearing the rockery in the Succulent Garden, I removed dozens of pretty regular bromeliads and planted them elsewhere, mostly along the trunk of a grand old Port Jackson fig, the others in a small area nearby. Lying in the garden was the weathered trunk of a large tree that had fallen long before I arrived here. We moved it to a position just under the fig and laid it on its side so the gnarled base stuck up appealingly into the air. It now serves not only as a structural element but as host to a small but interesting collection of epiphytes.

Move a little along the path and you'll encounter a number of old camellias emerging from the bank of clivias, many of them variegated – terribly unfashionable, I know, but I like them.

When still in my teens I had been taken to see Eryldene, the home of Professor E. G. Waterhouse and his wife, Janet. At that time, the mid-1950s, camellias were at the height of their popularity, with camellia societies flourishing, major shows up and down Sydney's north shore and a crowd-pulling one in the celebrated city retail store Farmer's. Even from my earliest exposure to this tree and its flowers, I have preferred the ones with variegated flowers. One of the most beautiful is *C. japonica* 'Paul Jones

ABOVE AND OPPOSITE: In this darker section of the garden, much use is made of striped and variegated plants. Above, campelia (*Tradescantia zanonia*), and opposite, *Alpinia zerumbet* 'Variegata' and the ground cover *Vinca major* 'Variegata' line a rustic set of stone steps.

Supreme', named after the botanical artist and Waterhouse's great friend. I have it growing here together with other striped and blotched varieties.

A little further along this walk you encounter some wonderful begonias, all grown from cuttings of specimens collected in the wild in south-west China by that most intrepid and generous of plantsmen Bob Cherry, while on one of his regular camellia-collecting expeditions. Visitors who think of begonias as limited in range are pleasantly surprised as they walk under plants taller than they are from which dangle absurdly large flowers in every imaginable form: white and yellow like popcorn, pink clusters like apple blossom, and dazzling whites and reds. If the variety of flower form is impressive, then the leaf forms are even more so: dappled paisley lozenges; flat circles of pale green speckled with yellow, resembling the size and appearance of rustic Italian plates; and large, red-backed, five-fingered forms with pinked edges. I have lost count of the number and none have names. Despite their exotic provenance, they look perfectly at home here, perhaps because this plant – of which there are some 900 varieties and numberless hybrids from Brazil, China, Mexico, Borneo and the Malay Peninsula, indeed almost all moist tropical countries except Australia – was a great favourite with Victorian gardeners. I do not grow the tuberous begonias used to such spectacular effect in private and public greenhouse displays throughout Australia. Instead, I've concentrated on the rhizomatous and tree forms, which do perfectly here.

Gingers are encountered on this walk, too: the lovely *Hedychium greenii* with its orange flowers and bronze-backed leaves that, with the light behind them, glow like molten metal; the so-called blue ginger (*Dichorisandra thyrsiflora*) with its luminous, inky flower clusters; and *Globba winitii*, promoted in the nursery trade as Thai ginger and with lovely drooping panicles, the upper bracts a rare and beautiful rose–purple from which emerges a saffron-coloured tubular corolla; plus a number of other varieties. Here, too, I grow hellebores, hydrangeas, marantas, in both the plain and variegated forms, zingoniums, cordylines and more brugmansias. A few wild cyclamens also flourish here, although I suspect they like it better at Olinda, in the Dandenongs, whence they came.

There are also three fine specimens of *Michelia doltsopa* planted at intervals along the downside of this walk. They look happy and healthy and have almost doubled in size since they were given to me as a moving-in present by yet another fine nurseryman, John Peck of Dural, but they have steadfastly refused to flower. Like the cyclamens, they are cold-climate plants, natives of Tibet, China and the Himalayas, and although the temperature in this shady lower area is noticeably cooler, several degrees lower than in the garden above, it is clearly not cold enough for them. A related plant, the champak (*Michelia champaca*), however, does very nicely at the eastern end of the walk, perhaps because it hails from India and Java but is now common throughout South-East

OPPOSITE AND ABOVE: The vast buttressed roots of a majestic Port Jackson fig sprawl over the rocks and travel almost 50 metres into adjoining soil. Probably seeded by a bird in a crevice, it is now of the most majestic size and form. To the left of it are clumps of bird's-nest ferns (*Asplenium australasicum*); in the centre, the bromeliads removed from the rockery; and in the fork of the tree, the Sydney rock lily (*Dendrobium speciosum* var. *hillii*), seen in flower above.

along the hidden path

Asia. Nosing its unique perfume, visitors are reminded of travels, for it is the scent of Bali and other romantic destinations.

I was lucky in this part of the garden to have a goodly supply of established trees and palms, in particular two splendid Canary Island date palms, but even luckier in the acquisition of no fewer than fourteen of their smaller cousins, *Phoenix robelinii*.

Few of us ever have any reason to thank banks, but I am grateful to Westpac. In 1996 I received a call from Mark Fitzgerald at Trade a Plant (see Resources, page 178). He had been summoned by the bank to remove seventeen *P. robelinii* palms from the bank's headquarters in Martin Place, and they had to be out within twenty-four hours. I had written about Fitzgerald's service, providing contacts for gardeners looking for mature specimens, and perhaps some bank official had seen the piece. The palms had been growing indoors in tubs dotted throughout the bank's foyers, so they were relatively easy to move. Within the allotted time (builders were due to move in immediately, hence the rush), the palms, all of various heights, were gathered, loaded onto a truck, delivered and planted in clumps along either side of this walk – another contributor to the mid-level canopy. In all, we calculated that these plants were worth about $10 000 retail – a nice gift from a bank that never had a cent's worth of my business.

Everything I have planted in this area of the garden is entirely imagined. There is not a shred of evidence to show what it looked like or if indeed it was ever cultivated. A narrow track runs along the other side of the fence, parallel to the one inside, but neither probably existed until relatively recently. My guess is that all of this area below the Carriageway Borders was natural bush with easy tracks along which ladies might easily move in long dresses. Or, for that matter, lovers.

While it's beyond the boundary of the property, the original Lovers' Walk is still of interest, particularly as a dedicated group of locals in the Bronte Gully Bush Regeneration Group has been working to restore the original planting here. The gully has, over the years, been invaded not only by barbaric camphor laurels but by coral trees and, bit by bit, the volunteers have been working to reintroduce native species. Norfolk Island pines, Port Jackson figs and other appropriate trees are planted in vast numbers – as they need to be, because all that can be afforded are seedlings and the mortality rate is high. If one stands on the front verandah of the house and looks east, one can see the fruits of their labour in the form of dozens of pale-blue plastic cylinders stretched around stakes to protect the infant plants from wind and salt. To be frank, the hill resembles a war cemetery, but in the long term some of the romantic appeal of the Lovers' Walk will have been returned to this once-sylvan gully.

ABOVE: Two of the various forms of clivia flourishing at Bronte: the common orange *C. miniata*, top, and *C. miniata* var. *citrina*, below.

OPPOSITE: Coy wild cyclamens and striped tradescantia. The former were a gift from alpine plant specialist Otto Fauser, and they flourish as happily here as they do in his celebrated garden at Olinda in Victoria's Dandenongs.

water

I had made two gardens before moving to Bronte House, both beautiful, but both with a serious deficiency. Neither had any form of what landscape designers like to call a 'water feature'. The garden at Bronte lacked one, too, although I was intrigued to find on an old map of the property an indicative position for one.

Back up at the beginning of the path to the lower garden, there was a circular bed that aroused suspicions. About 4 metres in diameter, it had a rolled edge constructed of brick and render. Now when nineteenth-century gardeners made circular beds, they usually simply cut them out of lawn, mounding the earth away from the circumference to clearly delineate the shape. The same technique applied to beds of any other form: squares, diamonds, long rectangles or the fashionable paisley shapes. Occasionally a bed might be edged with glazed terracotta tiles or ringed with lacy wirework, as though the flowers growing inside its circumference were spilling out of a basket, but cement edging was rare. Some detective work was called for.

The brickwork was in a sorry state and would need repair, and the planting within this large cement doughnut was uninspired – a collection of ailing arum lilies entirely unsuited to the soil condition. I decided to dig out the bed, repair the edging and replant, but when the time came to remove the soil, the remnants of an old pond were revealed. The cement floor of the pool had been fractured and corrugated by the roots of nearby trees, which is why somebody must have decided to fill it in and transform it into a bed. Better still, in the middle of the circle we discovered the sandstone footings for a fountain and even the rusted pipe that had once conveyed the water to it.

Given that the invasive figs nearby had already been removed and there was little chance of any further damage to a pond in this position, I began restoration. A local tradesman, Dave Piper, had observed the remnants of the structure when he visited on one of the early open days. Now that particular open day had been held to benefit the local public school and, as Dave had kids at the school and was appreciative of the support, he agreed to do the work on the pond at no cost. Not only did he do a superb job, he supplied some goldfish whose many offspring now move contentedly through the water.

Since there was little evidence of the form of the original fountain, I settled for a simple cast-iron copy of a mid-Victorian original, with a metal baluster and a small saucer mounted on top, into which water bubbles from the nozzle above before descending in long threads into the pond below. Just beneath the surface of the water, positioned on slabs of stone and neat plinths of brick, are terracotta pots of water-loving plants: the common arum lily (*Zantedeschia aethiopica*) and three varieties of the glorious Japanese water iris (*Iris ensata* 'Court Jester', 'Ocean Mist' and 'Stranger in Paradise'), familiar from

OPPOSITE: Visible from the Eastern Terrace, in the south-eastern corner of the garden, is the restored fountain. Its original six goldfish have multiplied many times and have managed to survive the depredations of resident kookaburras.

nineteenth-century prints, with flowers of veined purple and pink roughly the size of bread and butter plates. Water lilies grow here, too, and several types of surface weed to provide living camouflage from marauding kookaburras for the descendants of Dave Piper's fish.

This part of the garden was a kind of no man's land, hardly inviting inspection, so I set about improving it. There was evidence, in the form of sections of herringbone brick paving, that a path once encircled the pond, so that has been replaced and the excavated bricks used to form an edging.

A path leads from this little circular garden to a working area, and at each corner I set a multi-tiered quadrant-shaped Victorian wire plant stand. On these are placed the ultra-special hippeastrums, each in a simple pot made by T. Barker & Son, a long-established family pottery in the Sydney suburb of Granville (see Resources, page 178). Barker's were asked by the Historic Houses Trust of New South Wales to copy some old pots found at Elizabeth Farm, Parramatta. They did so and the result – hand-thrown, slightly irregular, tapered pots with thick rims that come with their own internally glazed saucers – are indistinguishable from antique ones when they get a little age on them. At the top of each stand is a small single pot, on the next shelf, three, then four, then five, then six, the sizes gradually getting bigger to accommodate bigger bulbs. The effect is a little like that of an eighteenth-century auricula theatre, the precious blooms displayed for maximum effect.

Few plants make so dramatic an impact as hippeastrums when brought indoors and while it's not easy to heave in the large ground-based pots with their multiple flowers, it's a simple matter to bring in these smaller pots and saucers and have the beautiful amaryllis blooming inside.

ABOVE TOP: The remnants of an original pond that we discovered after digging up a suspicious-looking bed. A square sandstone plinth on which a fountain once stood was uncovered, as were the old lead pipes that fed water to it.

ABOVE BOTTOM AND OPPOSITE: Waterlilies of three different colours – yellow, pink and blue – thrive in the pond.

It was soon clear that some sort of screen was needed between this small garden, with its rather Italianate air, and the work area that lay beyond. What I eventually settled for was yet another woven wire archway, smaller and narrower than the three installed in the upper garden. Over this rampages a Rangoon creeper (*Quisqualis indica*). Why this plant is not more widely grown is a mystery to me. The foliage – slender-pointed, ovate, lime-green leaves – is handsome and the flowers are sensational – simple five-petalled numbers each borne on a long spike and clustered in racemes.

Quisqualis is a compound of two Latin words – 'quis' meaning 'who' and 'qualis' meaning 'what kind'. Ostensibly this creeper was given the name because of original uncertainty as to the family of plants to which it belongs, but it could also have something to do with the fact that this delicious vine – the flowers of which have a fragrance like fruit salad – can't seem to make up its mind what colour it wants to be. Sometimes the flowers open white, sometimes pink, sometimes a combination of both colours, but mostly a wonderful dark garnet red. I am particularly proud of my Rangoon creeper plants; I raised them myself from cuttings taken from an old plant growing in the garden at Yasmar, an historic house at Haberfield in Sydney, now a prison for young offenders.

The work area was a bit of a shambles, really, and best not shown to visitors, crammed as it was with plant material waiting to be mulched, tree prunings, compost bins and the like. When Myles Baldwin first came to work here early in 2001, he was clearly itching to do some design work, and this was the last virgin area of the garden, the only part not already laid out. Myles conceived a plan, about which more will be revealed in the following pages.

OPPOSITE: Squadrons of lorikeets inhabit the garden at Bronte and use the fountain for ablutions.

ABOVE: The pond is now surrounded by cylindrical hand-thrown pots containing various kinds of hippeastrums.

along the hidden path

a flurry of frangipanis

Does any plant more potently evoke the languorous mood of summer in Sydney than the frangipani? The jacaranda, perhaps, but its magical flowers are fleeting and it lacks the frangipani's wonderful scent, which hangs so seductively in the air on warm nights.

The common white and yellow frangipani (*Plumeria rubra*), native to Panama and the area north to Mexico, is now to be found all over Asia. For obvious reasons, it became fashionable during the nineteenth century and was quickly appropriated by Australian amateur gardeners, becoming, by the turn of the century, a kind of badge of suburbia. Colonial mansions, Paddington terraces, Federation bungalows, holiday homes on the Central Coast, all had a mandatory specimen, usually planted by the front steps or close to a wall so the fragrance could be enjoyed by those entering the house or seated near an open window, which is where the one I inherited is planted at Bronte.

It does not show in a newspaper photograph of the house taken at the time of a visit by the then Premier, Sir Bertram Stevens, in 1935, but it must have been planted soon after, for this frangipani is now a big tree, beautiful when in flower and rather wonderful in winter, too, bare of branch and somewhat Jurassic, its strange, dense form like clusters of long liverwurst sausages. I have made the addition of a night-blooming cereus (*Hylocereus undatus*) that entwines its trunk and branches, slashing them with green and spangling them with flowers.

The Bronte frangipani was the ordinary one, with standard-issue yellow-centred white flowers. I like it, but it is not a favourite. It was, but that was before I discovered the range and beauty of less common varieties, and discovered that, in addition to different colours, there are different fragrances to these beautiful flowers, from coconut to fruit salad. The leaves can be different, too, the most beautiful form being the evergreen Singapore frangipani (*P. obtusa*), with whiter-than-white flowers and blunt paddle leaves of a beautiful dark green. Word has it that it can be grown in Sydney but I have never seen a specimen in this city, certainly not one as beautiful as I've seen in Broome or far north Queensland or Singapore.

Lovely as flowers of the common frangipani are, they can, if one is in a perverse frame of mind, seem a little like undersized poached eggs, whereas the exotic cultivars, ranging from pure white to pink to peach to bronze to darkest scarlet, are uniformly stunning.

Being a creature of obsessions I have, over the past decade, become obsessed by this plant, as have others. A lady frangipani fancier in Glebe who calls herself 'Carole the Cat Lover', and with whom I am in regular correspondence, has been a superior spotter. She even gathered cuttings in and around Broome and throughout the Northern Territory,

ABOVE AND OPPOSITE: Each frangipani 'acquired' for Bronte is identified by a silver tag indicating where it came from. Serious plantspersons sometimes get a shock to see a specimen identified as 'Rocky Point Road, Sans Souci'.

including a spectacular near-purple one from a tree growing beside a service station in Katherine, dispatching them to me in mailing tubes as she travelled. Whenever either of us spots a rare or unusual specimen growing in some suburban front- or backyard we e-mail each other and arrange a doorknock. Carole has collected sixty different colours and threatens to leave me her collection if and when she moves into an apartment. In the meantime I have, under my own steam, accumulated about thirty-eight varieties.

Eyes and nostrils open, I now notice every subtle variation and have even created a special computer folder in which I have listed every interesting mature tree that I've come across in Sydney: a pair of magnificent specimens with dusty-pink flowers flanking the steps leading up to an early-twentieth-century house in Petersham, some remarkable varieties in Earlwood grown from seed brought back from Darwin and Cairns . . . The chap who planted the trees in Earlwood was even able to supply a name for one of them – Herston Gem – which produces large pale-pink flowers. In Whale Beach I found a tree with large flowers blushed pink at the edges of the petals, shading to white and with the palest yellow centres. Again, this had been grown from special seed, in this case brought from New Guinea. The parent tree had been raised in Lane Cove and, when the family moved to the beach, large branches came with them to produce the current handsome specimen.

In my car I carry a pad and pencil and each time I spot a fine frangipani I make a note of the address and flower colour. Then, with a little more time than I had when making the original sighting, I return, usually in August when the tree is leafless and the form clearly visible. I simply knock on the door and ask for a piece. Most owners willingly oblige and usually with a respectable-sized cutting. But some owners can be tricky and mean. I take the view that in acquiring, by whatever means, a piece of a plant and propagating it, one is doing posterity a service, because without constant on-growing, many types and varieties of plants could disappear from the face of the earth. So if owners are not forthcoming then a midnight raid is an anti-social (and probably illegal) but time-honoured Aussie alternative. In fact, many plants in this garden have been begged, borrowed or nicked. I consider it 'sensitive theft' – an opinion formed after bitter experience.

A near neighbour had a superb red-flowered frangipani growing in their front garden, on a busy road and in full view of every pedestrian and passing car. Perhaps because it had always seemed too easy just to pop up and ask for a piece, I postponed doing so till I had collected cuttings from all the far-flung suburbs. Then one day I drove past to see that in the interests of constructing a brick fence, he or she (for I never met the owner to establish gender) had hacked the tree to the ground and, worse still, disposed of the loppings that might have brought joy to many gardeners.

Although I missed out on this beauty, I have obtained many wonderful cuttings

OPPOSITE AND ABOVE: Some of the different frangipanis from the collection at Bronte. Much work is being done by the recently formed Frangipani Society of Australia to identify properly each cultivar. Those thought to be unique to Australia will be designated by the additional appellation of 'Oz'.

locally. From a house in Clovelly came a magnificent one with sulphur-yellow flowers. From the back of a house in Carrington Street, Waverley, a brisk walk from Bronte House, came a marvellous one commonly called tutti-frutti. Others came from further away, from trees with bronze-coloured flowers in Milson's Point and Drummoyne, from a scarlet-flowered one in Balgowlah. The Drummoyne one is a particularly handsome example, with large flowers that have an intense scent rather like mango.

Upon acquisition by whatever means, begging or stealing, each cutting is labelled, identified by source – Wyrallah Road, Lismore; Stoney Creek Road, Bexley; Rainbow Street, Coogee and so on – on a small metal tag wired to the trunk and planted.

However, some remain elusive. There is, in Surry Hills, an amazing one that I lust for. From a distance this frangipani seems to produce orange flowers. In fact, it's a subtle blend of apricot and yellow flecked with pink and, in terms of the layering of colour, exactly resembles a peach, one colour overlaid on another to produce a third. I haven't got this one yet but will return one day, knock on the door and ask for a sizeable cutting. Maybe even offer ready money for a branch.

If someone is willing to give you a large piece, so much the better, for it can be stuck straight into the ground and you'll have, in effect, an instant tree. Mingier bits need to be coddled in a pot. Frangipanis are famously easy to strike and are relatively fast-growing but there are a few tips that may be useful. Grab a cutting whenever you can, but strictly speaking they are best taken in winter from leafless trees and left lying in a dry place, outdoors in the sun if the weather is warm, until a thin skin forms over the wound at the point where it was detached from the tree. Depending on the weather, this can take a couple of weeks, but I have successfully struck cuttings that have been lying around for a month or two. If it's wet, keep the cutting undercover. Then poke the stick into a pot of sandy loam. Roots should form in a month or two and in October the cutting will be ready to plant out.

Some of the frangipanis at Bronte have been grown in a slightly unusual way, stuck into crevices in the rocky section of the garden, allowed to branch out laterally or at odd angles and often underplanted with orchids, but grown this way they need staking. After a time, my collection of frangipanis large and small, identified only by swing labels with addresses written on them, and planted higgledy-piggledy in an out-of-the-way spot near the compost bins, grew so large that something needed to be done.

Myles Baldwin came up with an idea for a section of the garden dedicated to frangipanis, a kind of frangipani grove. The notion was an inspired one and, given the tiny planting space in which he had to work, he created a small masterpiece. First he cleared out the area in which the cuttings had been growing fitfully, removing bananas and palms to allow enough sun for growth. Then he devised a simple plan involving a tear-shaped central bed with a path on either side and with small, oddly shaped beds to

ABOVE AND OPPOSITE: The large frangipani in the centre of the photograph was here when I came to Bronte House and probably for a long time before that. The commonest of all frangipanis, *P. rubra* or *P. acutifolia* or *P. rubra* 'Acutifolia' – take your pick of botanical names, as the experts are yet to agree – can be found all over Australia and its fried-egg flowers (above) are no less beautiful for being ubiquitous.

the left and right. In the most conspicuous spot, he planted one of the loveliest of my collection, a large-flowered variety with unusually big, lolly-pink blooms and mandarin centres acquired from a garden in Castlecrag and brought to my attention by the well-known painter and decorator John Maestri, who has also been bitten by the frangipani bug. Around this striking centrepiece, Myles deployed the remainder of the collection, all different sizes, all different colours, some still in pots, some big enough to plant out. The cuttings continue to flow and the collection expands. We have run out of space but keep squeezing in more; sooner or later there will have to be a cull, a removal of some to another site.

In a sense, this concentration on collecting varieties of the one kind of plant – frangipanis, crinums and cannas – has been, for me, one of the greatest pleasures of this garden.

So there it is. Eight years' worth of work, some heartbreak, lots of joy – a garden remade and now throbbing with life. I have been told I have too many plants and should 'edit' them, but in truth there is little growing here that I could bear to be without.

Occasionally, forlorn under some more vigorous plant, I find something planted five or six years ago, long forgotten. Remembering what I hoped it might do, I carefully lift it and place it elsewhere. Some bulbs lie doggo for a year or two, then come rampaging out of the earth to surprise me and prompt a fresh view on placement. During the annual slash and burn in winter, lurking treasures are discovered, such as the tiny cyclamen given to me by Otto Fauser from Olinda in Victoria's Dandenong Ranges. They remind me of my visits to his lovely garden stuffed with alpine plants, and it pleases me to think that, of the myriad plants he can grow, there is this one that thrives so far north in a far warmer climate.

This is a garden of memories. Every plant here has a tale to tell, of acquisitiveness, happenstance, obsession or personal association. As I write this, the glorious crinum for which I made a special trip to Broome has come into flower for the first time. It is a marvel, its flowers huge, its clustered buds like shiny cerise cigars. All who walk through the gate stop to admire it, and for me it brings back the memory of digging it up from that public park in incandescent heat, lugging it back to my hotel, washing off the soil under the shower, trimming off its leaves with secateurs bought at the local hardware shop, wrapping it in a tarp purchased at the same time and lugging it back home. And its splendid florescence and obvious content at being here also reminds me of why I garden.

OPPOSITE: Unnamed frangipani cultivars are identified only by source. This one I simply call 'Kirribilli' frangipani.

ABOVE TOP: 'Coogee' frangipani.

ABOVE BOTTOM: 'Petersham' frangipani.

plant list

Plant lists are notoriously tricky things to compile. As specimens have been acquired, I've noted their names on a computer file, but a good deal of material I've gathered is either unnamed or the nomenclature is disputed. Nurseries have a habit of applying names – often cute ones – to plants and these tend to stick, sometimes marginalising or replacing botanical names. This master list comprises mainly common names of plant genera and may cover several species and sub-species.

  Echium is a case in point. While most cultivated blue echiums are variants of *E. candicans*, specific names have been applied to a particular colour, for instance, pride of Madeira. I have this, but I also have other unnamed blues that, although not an exact colour match, are clearly related. On the other hand, there are echiums that bear no resemblance to the blue Madeiran species. My point is that the repertoire of plants is ever-evolving; however, I have listed them in the clearest way I know.

NOTE ON ABBREVIATIONS

cv./cvs = cultivar/cultivars
f. = forma
spp. = species
sspp. = subspecies
syn. = synonymous
var. = variety
× = cross, hybrid

Botanical name	Common name

ANNUALS AND BIENNIALS

Alcea rosea 'Nigra' (syn. 'Black Beauty')	hollyhock
Anthriscus sylvestris	Queen Anne's lace
Centaurea cyanus 'Black Ball'	cornflower
Cleome (syn. *Sesquiorygalis*) *hassleriana* cvs 'Alba', 'Purple Queen'	spider flower
Cosmos bipinatus cvs 'Candy Stripe', 'Daydream', 'Picotee', 'Purity'	cosmos
C. sulphureus 'Bronte House'	yellow cosmos
Digitalis purpurea cvs 'Primrose Carousel', 'Sutton's Apricot'	foxglove, digitalis
D. purpurea f. *albiflora*	white foxglove
D. purpurea Gloxinioides Group cv. 'The Shirley'	foxglove
Eschscholzia californica	Californian poppy
Glaucium flavum	yellow-horned poppy
Helianthus annuus cvs 'Abendsonne', 'Indian Blanket', 'Moonwalker', 'Velvet Queen'	sunflower
Lathyrus odoratus cvs 'Captain of the Blues', 'Chatsworth', 'King-size Navy Blue', 'Matucana', 'Midnight', 'Orange Dragon', 'Painted Lady'	sweet pea
Nicotiana sylvestris and cvs 'Fragrant Cloud', 'Merlin White'	flowering tobacco
Papaver paeoniflorum	peony-flowered poppy
P. rhoeas	Flanders poppy
P. 'Thunder Cloud'	poppy
Plectranthus scutellarioides cvs 'Dragon Sunset', 'Fashion Parade', 'Palisandra', 'Volcano'	coleus
Tropaeolum majus cvs 'Empress of India', 'Peach Melba', 'Tip Top Apricot'	nasturtium
Zinnia 'Candy Cane'	zinnia

PERENNIALS

Acanthus mollis	oyster plant
Agapanthus cvs 'Albo-roseus', 'Dutch Giant'	agapanthus
A. inapertus 'Inky Tears'	agapanthus
Ajuga reptans cvs 'Caitlin's Giant', 'Jungle Beauty', 'Silver Carpet'	
Alocasia macrorrhiziza	elephant's ear
Alpinia zerumbet (syn. *A. nutans*) and cv. 'Variegata'	shell ginger
Alstroemeria cvs 'Inca Dream', 'Inca Salsa', 'Moonlight'	Peruvian lily
Angelica gigas	angelica
Aquilegia alpina 'Braveheart'	alpine columbine
A. cvs 'Crimson Star', 'Magpie'	columbine
Arabis blepharophylla 'Spring Charm'	California rock cress
Arctotis 'Cherry Velvet'	African daisy
Argyranthemum maderense	daisy
Aristea major	aristea
Artemisia arborescens 'Faith Raven'	wormwood
Bergenia cordifolia cvs 'Bressingham White', 'Olinda'	bergenia
Calathea veitchiana	
Canna brasiliensis	canna
C. edulis (a cv. of *C. indica*)	canna
C. × *generalis* cvs 'Aida', 'America', 'Der Rosenkavalier', 'Judy Cuppaidge', 'La Traviata', 'Madam Butterfly', 'Margerie Cole', 'Pink Sunburst', 'Rigoletto', 'Roi Humbert', 'Tropical Rose', 'Tropical Rose' (red form), 'Tropicana', 'Verdi', 'Warszewiczii', 'Wyoming'	canna
C. glauca	canna
C. indica 'Pretoria' (syn. 'Striatum', *malawiensis* 'Variegata', 'Bengal Tiger', 'Panaché')	canna
C. iridiflora	canna
Cistus aldibus	rock rose
C. 'Bennets White'	rock rose
Clivia miniata cvs 'Lutea', 'Sahin's Yellow', 'Variegata', 'Vico Yellow'	yellow clivia
C. miniata Belgian Hybrids	hybrid clivia
C. miniata var. *citrina*	citrina clivia
C. nobilis	drooping clivia
Colocasia esculenta 'Black Magic'	elephant's ear
Convolvulus cneorum	bush morning glory
Coreopsis grandiflora 'Early Sunrise'	tickseed
Crinum asiaticum	poison bulb
C. augustum	Queen Emma lily, spider lily
C. mauritianum	Cape Dawn
C. moorei	Moore's crinum
C. pacificum	crinum
C. pedunculatum	swamp crinum
C. × *powellii* and var. *alba*	Cape lily
Ctenanthe lubbersiana 'Bamburata'	ctenanthe
C. oppenheimiana 'Tricolor'	ctenanthe
Dahlia cvs 'Bishop of Llandaff', 'Cruden Farm', 'Dandy', 'Festival', 'Heat Seeker', 'Yellow Hammer'	dahlia
D. coccinea	Mexican dahlia
D. excelsa (syn. *D. imperialis*)	tree dahlia
Dianthus knappii	dianthus
Dichorisandra reginae	blue ginger
D. thyrsiflora	blue ginger
Dracunculus vulgaris	dragon lily
Echinacea purpurea and cv. 'Alba'	coneflower
Echinops bannaticus 'Taplow Blue'	globe thistle
Echium candicans (syn. *E. fatuosum*)	pride of Madeira
E. pininana	echium

E. simplex	echium
E. wildprettii	tower of jewels
Elettaria cardamomum	cardamom
Epilobium canum (syn. Zauschneria californica)	Californian fuchsia
Erigeron karvinskianus	seaside daisy
E. 'Quakeress'	
Eryngium agavifolium	sea holly
E. pandanifolium	sea holly
E. yuccifolium	sea holly
Eupatorium purpureum ssp. maculatum 'Gateway'	joe pye weed
Euphorbia mellifera	honey spurge
Foeniculum vulgare 'Purpureum'	bronze fennel
Fuchsia boliviana	fuchsia
Gaura lindheimeri	gaura
Gazania cvs 'Irish Eyes', 'White Opal'	gazania
Geranium 'Kashmir White'	geranium
G. maderense	geranium
Globba winitii	Thai ginger
Hedychium coccineum	red ginger lily
H. coronarium	ginger lily
H. greenii	ginger
Helleborus orientalis cvs 'Otto's Plum', 'Winter Rose'	hellebore
Hemerocallis cvs 'Custom Design', 'Doll House', 'Velvet Shadow'	day lily
Hibiscus glaber	hibiscus
H. trionum 'Sunny Days'	flower of an hour
Hymenocallis caribea	spider lily
Incarvillea arguta	incarvillea
Iresine herbstii	beefsteak plant, bloodleaf
Iris 'Dural White Butterfly'	Louisiana iris
I. ensata cvs 'Court Jester', 'Ocean Mist', 'Stranger in Paradise'	Japanese water iris
I. germanica	plain purple iris
I. japonica (syn. I. fimbriata)	crested iris
I. 'Night Edition'	bearded iris
I. pallida cvs 'Argentea Variegata', 'Variegata'	bearded iris
I. sibirica	Siberian iris
I. xiphium	Dutch iris
Kniphofia cvs 'Little Maid', 'Maid of Orleans'	red-hot poker
Leucanthemum × superbum cvs 'Aglaia', 'Snow Lady'	shasta daisy
Leucophyta brownii (syn. Calocephalus brownii)	cushion bush
Lobelia splendens 'Elmfeuer' ('Elmfire') (syn. L. fulgens)	scarlet lobelia
Lychnis × haageana (syn. L. × arkwrightii) 'Vesuvius'	campion
Malva 'Rix Phillips'	malvastrum
Musa acuminata 'Dwarf Cavendish'	
M. ensete (syn. Ensete ventricosum)	ensete
M. ornata	ornamental banana
M. velutina	self-peeling banana, pink banana
M. zebrina	striped-leaf banana
Oenothera deltoides var. howellii	Antioch Dunes evening primrose
O. 'Innocence'	evening primrose
O. speciosa 'Rose of Heaven'	evening primrose
Pelargonium tomentosum	peppermint geranium
P. triste	pelargonium
Perovskia atriplicifolia 'Longin'	Russian sage
P. neochilus 'Blue Spire'	Russian sage
Phlomis tuberosa	phlomis
Phormium cookianum cvs 'Tricolor', 'Yellow Wave'	flax
P. tenax Purpureum Group cvs 'Anna Red', 'Bobby Dazzler' (syn. 'Dazzler'), 'Dancer', 'Guardsman', 'Maori Maiden',	
'Platt's Black'	New Zealand flax
Plectranthus argentatus	native plectranthus
P. purpuratus	plectranthus
Ricinus communis 'Atropurpureum'	castor oil plant
Rudbeckia californica 'California'	rudbeckia
Salvia cvs 'Black Knight', 'Indigo Spires', 'Purple Majesty'	salvia, sage
S. chamaedryoides	germander sage
S. leucantha	Mexican bush sage
S. microphylla 'Iced Lemon'	little-leaf sage
S. sinaloensis	electric blue sage
Sedum cvs 'Herbstfreude' ('Autumn Joy'), 'Vera Jameson'	sedum
Silene banksias (syn. Lychnis × arkwrightii, L. × haageana) 'Vesuvius'	campion
Strelitzia nicolai	giant bird of paradise
S. reginae and cv. 'Mandela's Gold' and var. juncea	bird of paradise
Stromanthe sanguinea	stromanthe
Teucrium fruticans	bush germander
Tithonia diversifolia	tree marigold
T. rotundifolia	Mexican sunflower
Tulbaghia violacea 'Silver Lace'	variegated society garlic
Verbena 'Homestead Purple'	verbena
Viola hederacea	Australian violet
V. odorata	sweet violet
V. tricolor	Johnny jump up
Wachendorfia paniculata	red root
Zantedeschia aethiopica and cvs 'Green Goddess', 'Pink Mist'	arum lily

BULBS

Allium acuminatum	purple-flowered garlic
Crocosmia × crocosmiiflora 'Lucifer'	montbretia
C. potksii 'Solfatare'	montbretia
Eucharis × grandiflora	eucharist lily
Haemanthus albiflos	blood lily
H. coccineus	blood lily
Hippeastrum cvs 'Apple Blossom', 'Bouquet', 'Mont Blanc', 'Papilio', 'Picotee'	hippeastrum
Lilium Asiatic Hybrids 'Candy Dulfer', 'Cannes', 'Lollipop', 'Marakech', 'Massa'	Asiatic lilies
L. formosanum	Formosa lily
L. henryi	lilium
L. longiflorum	November lily
L. Oriental Hybrids 'Black Beauty', 'Casablanca', 'Devotion', 'Early Rose', 'Maharajah', 'Miss Rio', 'Rubbrovittatum Apollo', 'Siberia', 'Taj Mahal', 'Top Choice'	oriental lilies
L. regale	regal lily
Nectaroscordum siculum (syn. Allium siculum)	Sicilian honey garlic
Oxalis debilis	flowering oxalis
Sprekelia formosissima	Jacobean lily
Watsonia meriana	watsonia
Worsleya procera (syn. W. rayneri)	worsleya, Empress of Brazil
Zephyranthes candida	autumn crocus

CLIMBING PLANTS AND GROUND COVER

Antigonon leptopus	coral vine
Aristolochia gigantea	giant Dutchman's pipe
Beaumontia grandiflora	beaumontia
Bougainvillea glabra 'Magnifica'	purple bougainvillea
Convolvulus cvs 'Milky Way', 'Star of Yalta'	morning glory
Humulus lupus 'Aureus'	golden hop
Hylocereus undatus	night-blooming cereus

Ipomoea lobata	mina lobata
Jasminum azoricum	lemon-scented jasmine
Lathyrus odoratus	sweet pea (*see also* 'ANNUALS')
Lonicera hildebrandiana	giant honeysuckle
L. 'Cuppaidge Pink'	honeysuckle
Marsdenia floribunda (syn. *Stephanotis floribunda*)	Madagascar jasmine, stephanotis
Pandorea pandorana	wonga wonga vine
Pyrostegia venusta	orange trumpet vine
Quisqualis indica	Rangoon creeper
Syngonium 'Green Butterfly'	arrowhead vine
Tecomanthe hillii	Fraser Island creeper
Thunbergia coccinea	red thunbergia
T. grandiflora and cv. 'Alba'	sky flower
T. mysorensis	Indian thunbergia
Trachelospermum jasminoides	Chinese star jasmine
Tradescantia fluminensis	wandering Jew
T. zanonia	campelia
Vigna caracalla	snail vine
Vinca major 'Variegata'	variegated periwinkle
Wisteria brachybotrys 'Shiro Kapitan'	silky wisteria
W. floribunda cvs 'Kuchibeni', 'Shiro Noda', 'Violacea Plena'	Japanese wisteria
W. sinensis and cvs 'Alba', 'Rosea'	Chinese wisteria

GRASSES, BAMBOOS AND SEDGES

Bambusa balcooa	baluka bamboo
B. multiplex 'Alphonse Karr'	bamboo
Carex riparia	pond sedge
Calamagrostis acutifolia	stricta
C. × acutiflora 'Karl Foerster'	feather reed grass
Imperata cylindrica 'Rubra'	Japanese blood grass
Miscanthus sinensis cvs 'Sarabande', 'Silberfeder' ('Silver Feather'), 'Variegatus', 'Zebrinus'	eulalia
Ophiopogon japonicus	mondo grass
O. planiscapus 'Nigrescens'	black mondo grass
Pennisetum setaceum 'Burgundy Giant'	fountain grass
Pleioblastus spp. *Arundinaria*	dwarf bamboo
Stipa gigantea	golden oats
S. tenacissima	esparto grass
S. tenuissima	
Themeda gigantea	ulla

ORCHIDS

Cirrhopetalum fasciatum	cirrhopetalum
Cymbidium cvs 'Emerald Downs', 'Gowendale', 'Summer Cloud'	cymbidium orchid
Dendrobium kingianum	pink rock orchid
D. speciosum var. *hillii*	Sydney rock lily, king orchid
Epidendrum ibaguense cvs 'Coral Lea', 'King Lavender', 'Purple Heart'	crucifix orchid
Zygopetalum intermedium	zygopetalum

SHRUBS

Brugmansia aurea	yellow angel's trumpet
B. cvs 'Charles Grimaldi', 'Frosty Pink'	angel's trumpet
B. rosea	angel's trumpet
B. sanguinea	red angel's trumpet
B. tomentosa	angel's trumpet
B. versicolor	angel's trumpet
Buddleia brevifolia × *B. davidii*	buddleia
B. davidii 'Lutea'	buddleia
B. × *weyeriana* cvs 'Golden Glow', 'Trewithen'	buddleia
Buxus microphylla	box
B. sempervirens	English box
Camellia japonica cvs 'Aspasia Macarthur', 'Carter's Sunburst', 'Contessa Lavinia Maggi', 'Courtesan', 'Dona Herzilia de Freitas Magalhaes', 'Magnoliaflora', 'Nuccio's Gem', 'Paul Jones Supreme'	japonica camellia
C. sasanqua	camellia
Cestrum nocturnum	night-blooming cestrum
Citrus reticulata 'Emperor'	mandarin
Clerodendrum serratum	clerodendrum
Cordyline fruticosa	cordyline
Datura inoxia (syn. *D. meteloides*, *Brugmansia meteloides*)	white thorn apple
Dietes robinsoniana	Lord Howe Island wedding flower
Doryanthes excelsa	Gymea lily
Dracaena marginata and cv. 'Tricolor'	dracaena
Gardenia augusta 'Florida'	gardenia
Heliotropium arborescens cvs 'Alba', 'Lord Roberts', 'Marine'	cherry pie
Hibiscus tiliaceus	seaside hibiscus
Hydrangea macrophylla 'Maculata'	variegated lace-cap hydrangea
Mackaya bella	forest bell bush
Medinilla myrantha	medinilla
Melianthus major	honey bush
Murraya exotica (syn. *M. paniculata*)	murraya
Mussaenda frondosa	mussaenda
Nerium oleander cvs 'Madame Charles Baltet', 'Mademoiselle Du Bois', 'Sue Hawley Oakes'	oleander
Osteospermum	African daisy
O. ecklonis	sailor-boy daisy
Rhododendron Vireya Group 'Orange Wax'	vireya
Rosmarinus officinalis	rosemary
Synadenium compactum	African milk bush
Trevesia sundaica	

ROSES

Rosa chinensis and cv. 'One Thousand Lights'	China rose
R. cvs 'Crépuscule', 'Ferdinand Pichard', 'Greensleeves', 'Ingeborg Charlotte', 'Lady Hillingdon', 'Mutabilis', 'Pierre de Ronsard'	
David Austin's Rose Group: *Rosa* cvs 'Abraham Darby', 'Charles Austin', 'David Austin', 'Ellen', 'Emanuel', 'Graham Thomas', 'Jayne Austin', 'Lilac Rose', 'Moonbeam', 'Pat Austin', 'Symphony', 'Troilus', 'Wildflower', 'Windrush', 'Yellow Charles Austin'	**David Austin's English roses**

CACTI AND SUCCULENTS

Aeonium arboreum var. *atropurpureum*	
A. 'Schwarzkopf'	
Agave var. *marginata*	century plant
A. americana var. *mediopicta*	century plant
A. attenuata	agave
A. parryii	agave
A. stricta	royal agave
A. victoriae-reginae	royal agave
Aloe jacksonii	aloe
A. plicatilis	fan aloe
A. saponaria	soap aloe
A. × *spinosissima* (*A. humilis* × *A. arborescens*)	aloe

A. striata	aloe
Cereus uruguayanus 'Monstrosus'	apple cactus
Cotyledon orbiculata	pig's ear
C. undulata	cotyledon
Crassula arborescens	crassula
C. multicava	fairy crassula
C. ovata	jade plant
C. perfoliata var. *minor*	propeller plant
Cyphostemma juttae	
Disocactus × *hybridus*	epiphyllum
Echeveria agavoides	
E. cvs 'Black Prince', 'Pink Form'	
E. elegans	
E. × *imbricata*	
Euphorbia hyberna	euphorbia
E. trigona and var. 'Red Devil'	African milk bush
Furcraea selloa	furcraea
Gasteria ernesti-ruschi	
Haworthia pumila	
Kalanchoe beharensis	velvet elephant ear
K. blossfeldiana	flaming katy
K. delagoensis (syn. *K. tubifolia*)	
K. marmorata	
Ledebouria socialis	scilla violacea
Neobuxbaumia euphorbioides	cactus
Pachypodium lamerei	Madagascar palm
P. rosulatum	mini-baobab
Portulaca hybriod	pig's face
Sansevieria singularis	
S. trifasciata and cv. 'Laurentii'	mother-in-law's tongue
Sedum 'Aurora'	stonecrop
S. hispanicum	stonecrop
S. nudum	sedum
S. pachyphyllum	jellybean plant
S. rubrotinctum	sedum
S. telephium spp. *ruprechtii*	orphine
Selaginella kraussiana	selaginella
Sempervivum cvs 'Lavender', 'Royal Ruby', 'Topaz'	houseleek
S. tectorium	common houseleek
Senencio cowleyanus	string of beads
S. serpens	blue chalk stick
Yucca filamentosa 'Variegata'	Adam's needle
Y. 'Purpureum'	purple-leaved yucca

TREES

Acmena smithii	lilly pilly
Agathis robusta	Queensland kauri pine
Araucaria bidwillii	bunya pine
A. columnaris	araucaria

A. heterophylla	Norfolk Island pine
Archontophoenix × *cunninghamiana*	bangalow palm
Bismarckia nobilis	Bismarck palm
Brachychiton discolor	lacebark
Butia capitata	Brazilian wine palm
Catalpa bignonioides	Indian bean tree
Chorisia speciosa (syn. *Ceiba speciosa*)	silk floss tree
Dracaena draco	dragon tree
Erythrina crista-galli	coral tree, cock's comb
Ficus microcarpa var. *hillii*	Hill's weeping fig
F. rubiginosa	Port Jackson fig
Howea belmoreana	curly palm
H. fosteriana	kentia palm
Latania lontaroides	red latan palm
Liriodendron tulipifera	tulip tree
Lophostemon confertus	brush box
Magnolia grandiflora and cv. 'Exmouth'	magnolia
M. × *loebneri* 'Merill'	Loebner magnolia
M. macrophylla	big leaf magnolia
Michelia alba	michelia
M. champaca	champak
M. doltsopa	michelia
Pandanus peduncularis	screw pine
Phoenix canariensis	Canary Island date palm
P. roebelinii	dwarf date palm
Plumeria obtusa	Singapore frangipani
P. rubra f. *acutifolia* and cvs	frangipani
Podocarpus elatus	brown pine
Randia fitzalanii	native gardenia
Raphis excelsca	lady palm
Spathodea campanulata	African tulip tree
Tibouchina lepidota 'Alstonville'	Alstonville tibouchina

FERNS

Asplenium australiasicum and cv. 'Victoria'	bird's-nest fern
Blechnum nudum	fishbone water fern
Chamaedorea costaricana	
Cyathea cooperi	tree fern
Dicksonia antarctica	soft tree fern
Doodia	
Pteris umbrosa	ribbon fern
Woodwardia radicans	

NOTABLE BROMELIADS

Hohenbergia corriao-arauji	
Neoregalia 'Johannes Royal Burgundy'	
Vriesea hieroglyphica	

resources

T. Barker & Son
5 A'Beckett Street
Granville NSW 2142
Tel: 02 9637 1891
Fax: 02 9637 7232

Canna Brae Country Garden Nursery
35–37 Felix Crescent
Ringwood North VIC 3134
Tel: 03 9870 1130

Charlie's Compost
Charlie and Rose Hamand
656 George Downes Drive
Kulnura NSW 2250
Tel: 02 4376 1202

Cloudehill Nursery and Garden Centre
89 Olinda-Monbulk Road
Monbulk VIC 3793
Tel: 03 9751 1009

Digger's Seeds
105 La Trobe Parade
Dromana VIC 3936
Tel: 03 5987 1877
Fax: 03 5981 4298

Impact Plants
Poole Close
Empire Bay NSW 2257
Tel: 02 4369 1422
Fax: 02 4369 1485

Lambley Nursery
'Burnside'
Lesters Road
Ascot VIC 3364
Tel: 03 5343 4303
Fax: 03 5343 4257
www.lambley.com.au

The Perfumed Garden
Nepean Highway
Mt Martha VIC 3934
Tel: 03 5974 4833
Fax: 03 5974 8455

Pine Grove Nursery
114 Pine Street
Wardell NSW 2477
Tel: 02 6683 4188

Thompson & Morgan UK
Poplar Lane
Ipswich, Suffolk
UK IP8 3BU
Tel: +44 (0) 1473 688 821
Fax: +44 (0) 1473 680 199
www.thompson-morgan.com

Trade a Plant
Level 1/148 Wycombe Road
Neutral Bay NSW 2089
Tel: 02 9904 4000
Fax: 02 9904 4003
www.tradeaplant.com.au

Vaucluse House
Wentworth Road
Vaucluse NSW 2030
Tel: 02 9388 7922
Fax: 02 9337 4963
www.hht.nsw.gov.au

For details of open days at Bronte House, see the website at **www.brontehouse.com**

acknowledgements

Many people have helped in the remaking of the garden at Bronte House, providing advice, information, manual labour, cuttings, rare plants, lawn clippings for the compost heap and, most importantly, encouragement and caution in equal measure. Rather than catalogue their individual contributions, I simply list them alphabetically: Dr James Broadbent, Don Burke, Glenn Callcott, Bob and Derelie Cherry, Errol and Patricia Cosh, Judy Cuppaidge, Peter Cuppaidge, Elizabeth Ellis, David Glenn and Criss Canning, John Happ, Ian Innes, Wayne Jury, Michael McCoy, Professor David Mabberley, Cheryl Maddocks, William Martin, Dave Piper, Steve Putnam, Bruce Rann, Jennifer Stackhouse, Howard Tanner and Carole von Aarberg. I offer them all grateful thanks on behalf of myself and the thousands who have visited and enjoyed Bronte House.

Julie Gibbs of Penguin urged me to write this book and, by alternately cajoling and badgering me, ensured its completion. Thanks to my editor Jane Morrow, designer Nikki Townsend, and to the talented, enthusiastic and altogether adorable Simon Griffiths who, over two and a bit years, faithfully recorded both the many failures and the occasional successes.

Thomas Engesser and his wife Alison Gill have been unfailingly supportive throughout the restoration and writing process, as have members of my family, and the current gardener, Myles Baldwin, gets as excited about the garden as I do.

My old and good friend Richard d'Apice, who also happens to be my lawyer, attempted to dissuade me from taking on the lease of Bronte House and the attendant responsibilities. He failed. 'It will be a sinkhole into which you pour money,' he warned me, as indeed it has proved to be. But the rewards have been vast and even he now grudgingly approves.

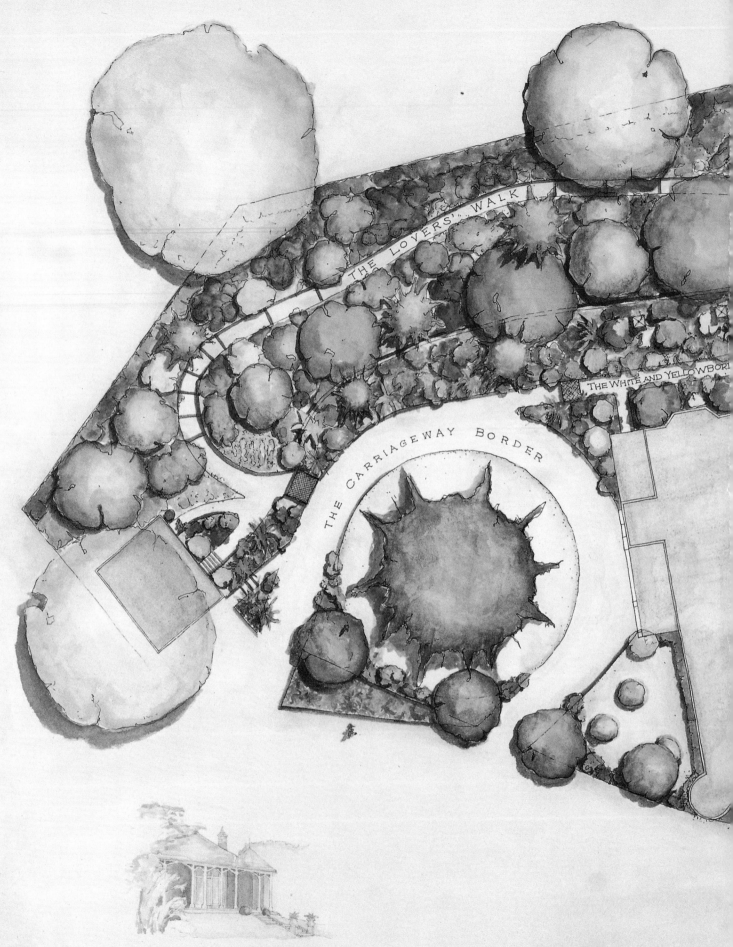

THE LOVERS' WALK

THE WHITE AND YELLOW BOR

THE CARRIAGEWAY BORDER

BRONTE HOUSE, BRONTE NSW